Selenium

With

Python

Simplified

A beginner's guide to Automation Testing using Python and Selenium Webdriver

Copyright © 2020 S Basu

All rights reserved.

Disclaimer:

The information and materials presented here are for educational purposes only. Every effort has been made to make this book as complete and as accurate as possible but no warranty or fitness is implied. The information provided is on an "as is" basis. The ideas and opinions expressed are of the author's own imagination and the author is not affiliated to any organization, school or educational discipline and will not be held accountable or liable for any inadvertent misrepresentation.

Contents

INTRODUCTION: 5

CHAPTER 1: HTML AND CSS 7
   1.1: INTRODUCTION TO HTML AND DOM 7
   1.2: INTRODUCTION TO CASCADING STYLE SHEETS (CSS) 9
      1.2.1: Internal CSS 10
      1.2.2: External CSS 23
      1.2.3: In-Line CSS 34

CHAPTER 2: INTRODUCTION TO PYTHON PROGRAMMING. 35
   2.1: PYTHON INSTALLATION 35
   2.2: PYTHON DATATYPE AND VARIABLES 40
   2.3: PYTHON LIST 42
   2.4: PYTHON TUPLE 43
   2.5: PYTHON DICTIONARY 44
   2.6: PYTHON CONTROL STATEMENTS 45
   2.7: PYTHON FUNCTIONS. 47
   2.8: PYTHON CLASS 48
   2.9: PYTHON INHERITANCE 51
   2.10: PYTHON TRY EXCEPT BLOCK 54

CHAPTER 3: SELENIUM 57
   3.1: SELENIUM WEBDRIVER ARCHITECTURE 58
   3.2: SELENIUM AND DRIVER INSTALLATION 59
      Example 1 61
   3.3: LOCATING WEB PAGE ELEMENTS 63
      Example 1 68
      Example 2 70
      Example 3 73
      Example 4 76
      Example 5 79
      Example 6 81
      Example 7 82
      Example 8 84
      3.3.1: XPATH 85
      Example 9 88

3.4: SELENIUM WAITS 94
   3.4.1: Implicit Wait 95
   3.4.2: Explicit Wait 95
3.5: SELENIUM PAGE OBJECT MODEL 99
   Page Object Model Architecture 100
   3.5.1: Base Page 100
   3.5.2: Locators 103
   3.5.3: Pages 104
   3.5.4: Test 108
   3.5.5: Test Suite 116
   3.5.6: How to generate a HTML report or a log file after running a Test Case Class 118

Introduction:

What is Automation Testing?

Automation testing is similar to Manual testing which involves vigorous end to end testing of the entire web application. But the only difference is that in Manual testing a person is manually testing the entire application but in Automation testing, the scripts developed by the Automation Programmers performs the testing for you.

Automation testing becomes extremely useful during **Regression testing** because it saves time and money.

What is Regression Testing?

Regression testing is performed on an existing application.

In various phases of the software development, new features often get added to the web application. Regression testing ensures that any newly added feature does not break the existing application. This is done by rerunning tests, both functional and non-functional tests on existing features.

As the name suggests, Automation Testing tools helps with automation. One feature is **record and playback button**. Record and playback captures the general flow of a web application. But Automation programmers usually avoid this feature and develop their own test scripts coded in different programming languages like **Java** or **Python**.

There are many Automation Testing tools available but among them the most popular one is **Selenium**.

Before we enter into **Selenium** topic, first we need to understand the basic structure of a web page and understand why web elements are assigned **ID** and **Class name** etc. Subsequently we need to understand the **Python programming language**. After completing these two topics, then we will proceed to **Selenium**.

So let's get started.

Chapter 1: HTML and CSS

1.1: Introduction to HTML and DOM

What is HTML?

HTML stands for Hyper Text Markup Language.

HTML elements help to design a web page and they are represented with open and close tags. Example: (open tag) < *element_name* > ...... </ *element_name* > (close tag)

```
              < html >
                 ⇓
    _____
       ⇓                    ⇓
    < head >             < body >
    </head>              </body>
```

HTML document is divided into **head** and the **body**.

The **<head>** contains all information about a web page. Example: CSS, Javascript, meta data

The **<body>** contains the main content of the web page which will get displayed to the user.

What is DOM?

DOM stands for Document Object Model which defines the logical structure of a document.
Let's look into a basic DOM structure below

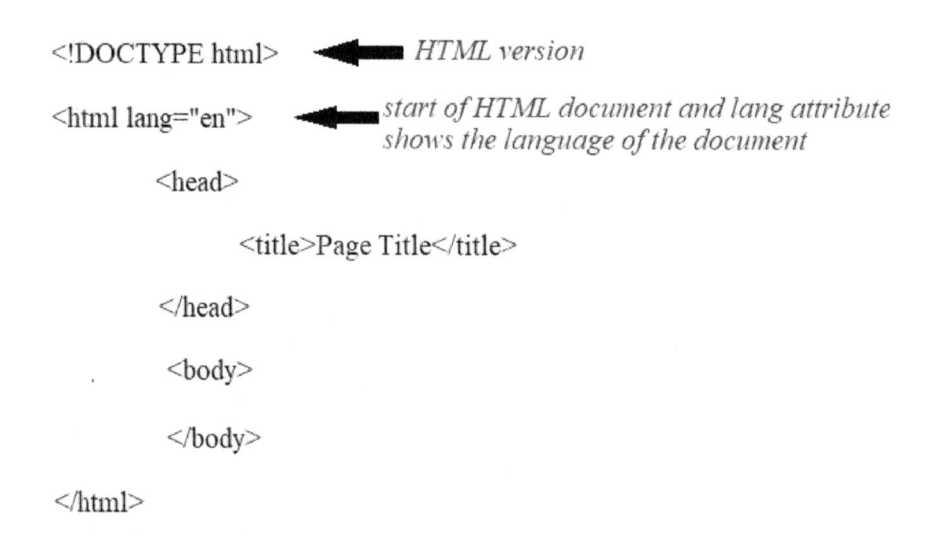

```
<!DOCTYPE html>          ⬅ HTML version

<html lang="en">         ⬅ start of HTML document and lang attribute
                            shows the language of the document
    <head>

        <title>Page Title</title>

    </head>

    <body>

    </body>

</html>
```

The DOM of above HTML code is:

```
            DOCUMENT
               ↓
              HTML
               ↓
        ┌──────┴──────┐
        ↓             ↓
       HEAD          BODY
        ↓
        ↓
      TITLE
```

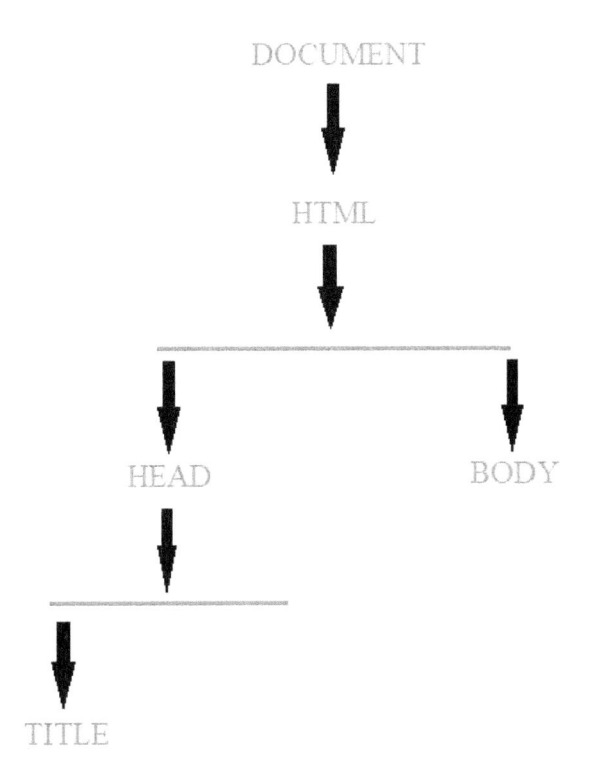

There are hundreds of HTML tags present. We will look into few important ones as we proceed further and start creating our web project.

1.2: Introduction to Cascading Style Sheets (CSS)

CSS stands for Cascading Style Sheets and is mainly used to make a HTML document pretty and presentable. If there are multiple pages using the same styling information, CSS helps us to save time by preventing repetitive work.

An HTML web element contains a number of attributes but among them the most important ones are the **ID** and the **Class name**. These attributes are not only important for locating the web element to perform automation testing, but it is also very important while adding CSS styling information.

CSS is of three types:

1. Internal CSS

2. External CSS

3. Inline CSS

1.2.1: Internal CSS

In Internal CSS, the CSS codes and main content of the web page are present within the same HTML document and it provides styling information exclusive for that page.

The CSS codes are written within the **<style>** tags in the **<head>** section of a HTML file.

```
<!DOCTYPE html>
<html lang="en">
    <head>
        <style>
            ↑
            | CSS codes
            ↓
        </style>
    </head>
    <body>
    </body>
</html>
```

Now let's start coding..

We will be creating a HTML document with Internal CSS. Open **Notepad** or **Notepad++** -> Create a New File and save it as HTML. Name the file *index.html*

In this book, we will be creating a project called *Tasty Home Food Delivery Service*. It is a simple project which will contain a *Home Page* and a *Create a new profile*. As we proceed further, we will be testing and automating this entire web application with the help of **Python** and **Selenium Webdriver**.

The link to my website:
http://sbasu.pythonanywhere.com/tastyFoodApp/

(***Please note:*** *I created this website mainly for Automation practice purpose only*)

Let's design our *Home page*.

index.html

```
<!DOCTYPE html>
<html>
<head>

<meta name="viewport" content="width=device-width, initial-scale=1.0">
<title>Tasty Home Food Delivery Service</title>

<style>
    body{
    background-image:url("C:/..../..._.../Picture4.jpg")
    background-repeat: repeat;
    width:100%;
    height:100%;
    }
</style>
</head>
<body>


</body>
</html>
```

- In above HTML code, I created a web page and gave it a **title** of *Tasty Home Food Delivery Service*.

- To add CSS styling information to the **<body>** of HTML document, go to **<head>** tag -> **<style>** tag -> within **<style>** tag call the HTML element by its tag name and give the desired styling information within the curly brackets { ….. }.

    o Added a **background image** to the <body> of the web page.

    The CSS code is:

    background - image : url (" *picture_location* **") ;**

13

- If we want the background image to **repeat** itself and fill the web page then the CSS code is:

    background-repeat: repeat;

- I have set the **height** and the **width** of the body of the web page to 100%.

NOTE: It is very important to set **height** and **width** of the **body** of a web page. This acts as a parent container and helps to prevent layout shifts of different elements present within the web page.

Now, let's give a **heading** to the *Home page*.

To add a heading, HTML provides us with **<h1>** tag

HTML

```
<body>
    <div id = "homePageHeader">
    <img id = "logoPic"
    src = "...\......\...' \Picture5.jpg" alt="Logo Pic">
    <h1>Tasty Home Food Delivery Service</h1>
    </div>
```

CSS

```
#homePageHeader{
margin-top:30px;
border:30px solid #808080;
background-color:white;
height:550px;
width:100%;
position:relative;
}

h1{
position:absolute;
top:0px;
left:380px;
font-family:Kristen ITC;
color:#404040;
font-weight:bold;
font-size:60px;
}

#logoPic{
float:left;
}
```

In the above HTML code,

- The **<div>** container with **id** *homePageHeader* holds both heading (**<h1>**) as well as the logo image with **id** *logoPic*.

The syntax for adding any image is:

< **img src** = " *image_location* " **alt**= " *image_name* " >

alt attribute is used to set an alternate text for the image, if the image fails to load.

What is Id in CSS?

ID helps to uniquely identify certain HTML elements. In order to access the **id** of an HTML element within **<style>** tag, a hashtag (#) symbol is used. Example: *# id_name*

What is <div> tag?

The **<div>** tag defines a division or a section in an HTML document. It is a good practice to divide different sections of a web page into different **<div>** containers.

To add styling information to the **<div>** container with **id** *homePageHeader,* **<h1>** and to **<image>** with **id** *logoPic*, go to the **<head>** section -> then within **<style>** tag call each HTML element by its tag name or **id** and give the desired styling information within the curly braces { ….. }.

- The CSS information added to **id** *homePageHeader* are:

    o **margin - top** sets the top margin to the **<div>** container to *30px*.

    o **border** sets a border around the **<div>** container. This property helps to specify the width and color of the border. The value **solid** means the border contains solid lines.

- **background - color** sets the color of the background of **<div>** container to *white*.

- We have declared the **<div>** container with **id** *homePageHeader* as the **parent container** and set its **position** to **relative**.

    position : relative

The CSS information added to **<h1>** tag are:

- We have declared the **<h1>** tag as child element of the **<div>** container with **id** *homePageHeader* and set its **position** to **absolute**.

    position : absolute

    Now the **<h1>** tag (*child element*) is positioned relative to the parent element. We have set the **top** of **<h1>** to *0px* and **left** to *380px*.

NOTE: In order to move a child element to the **bottom, top, left** or **right** we need to declare a parent element and a child element by using **position properties**.

- **font - family** sets the font used by **<h1>** tag to *Kristen ITC*.

- **color** sets the text color used by **<h1>** tag

- **font-weight** sets the boldness of the text used by <h1> tag

- **font-size** sets the size of the text used by <h1> tag

I would like to set the logo image with **id *logoPic*** on the **left** hand side of its parent container (**<div>** element with **id *homePageHeader***) and in order to do that we use CSS **float property**.

- **float : left**

What is float property?

The CSS float property is used to place an element to the **left** or **right** of its parent container.

Now let's save ***index.html*** and open the file using Google Chrome.

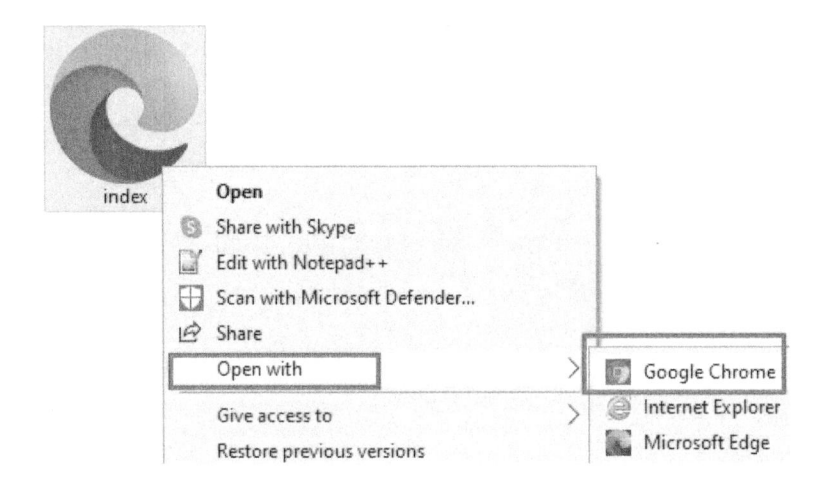

18

It looks perfect.

Now let's create a list of links which will enable a user to navigate to different pages.

For now we will be creating only one link that will lead us to a *Create a new profile* page.

HTML

```
<body>
    <div id = "homePageHeader">
    <img id = "logoPic"
    src = "...\...\...\...\Picture5.jpg" alt="Logo Pic">
    <h1>Tasty Home Food Delivery Service</h1>

    <div id = "homePageLinks">
    <ul>
    <li><a href = "....://CHTML/createNewProfile.html">Create New Profile</a></li>
    </ul>
    </div>
    </div>
```

CSS

```css
#homePageLinks{
position:absolute;
bottom:0px;
right:50px;
width:21%;
height:100px;
background-color:#cccccc;

}

li{
display: inline;
font-family:Verdana;
font-size:20px;
background-color:#808080;
padding:20px;
}

a{
text-decoration:none;
color:white;
}

li:hover{
background-color:orange;
}
</style>
</head>
```

In the above HTML code,

- We have created another **<div>** container with **id** *homePageLinks*, which holds the list of links. This container also acts as a child element of parent container with **id** *homePageHeader*.

To create any **list**, **<ul>** and **<li>** tags are needed.

The syntax is:
    <ul>
    <li> *item one* </li>
    <li> *item two* </li>
    .....
    </ul>

<ul> stands for **unordered list** and each items within the list should be present within **<li>** tags.

In order to make the links functional, **<a> href** attribute is needed. The syntax is:

< a href = " *..url...* "**>** *link_name* **</a>**

What is <a> tag and its href attribute?

<a> tag is used to define a hyperlink and its **href** attribute specifies the **url** of the page the link goes to.

In the above CSS code,

- We have declared *homePageLinks* as the child container and positioned it to the **bottom right** side of its parent container.

21

> **position : absolute**
>
> **bottom :** *0px*
>
> **right :** *50px*

- o I have also set the **height** and **width** of the container and gave a **background color**.

  > **background - color :** *color_name*;

- I would like the **<li>** tag within **<ul>** tag to be displayed side by side instead of one after another. In order to do that the **display** property is set to **inline**.

  > **display : inline;**

  For the **<a>** tag links, I have set its color and set the text-decoration to none.

  > **text-decoration : none;**

What is text-decoration property?

This CSS property specifies the decoration added to the text. By setting the **text-decoration** property to **none**, I was able to remove the underscore from the HTML link

---

- **:hover** selector is used to change color when a user hovers over that element.

  The code li : hover { background-color : *orange*; } specifies that turns the color of each **<li>** element to *orange* when a user hovers the mouse over it.

Now let's save everything and open *index.html* with Google chrome browser.

Everything looks good.

1.2.2: External CSS

Important points to note in External CSS are:

In External CSS, we write our CSS code in a separate file and link that file with our HTML document using **<link>** tag.

By separating the CSS code from HTML codes, makes the HTML document look cleaner and less complicated.

External CSS saves time and prevents repetitive work of writing the same CSS code for multiple pages.

Open **Notepad++** -> create a CSS file and I named my file *foodDelivaryCss.css*.

```
File name:     foodDelivaryCss
Save as type:  Cascade Style Sheets File (*.css)

Hide Folders
```

This CSS file contains the styling information for all HTML web elements that belong to CSS **Class** *container*, *fieldStyle*, *submitButton* and *backlink*.

foodDelivaryCss.css.

```css
body{
    background-image:url("C:/Users/PL./Picture4.jpg");
    background-repeat: repeat;
    width:100%;
    height:100%;
}
.container{
    margin-top:100px;
    background-color:#e68a00;
    width:50%;
    height:auto;
    margin-left:auto;
    margin-right:auto;
    font-family:Verdana;
    font-size:20px;
    color:white;
    position:relative;
}

.fieldStyle{
    width:300px;
    height:30px;
}
```

```css
.submitButton{
    position:absolute;
    bottom:0px;
    right:20px;
    width:100px;
    height:50px;
    background-color:#595959;
    color:white;
    font-family:Verdana;
    font-size:15px;
    font-weight:bold;
}
.submitButton:hover{
    background-color:orange;
}

.backLink{
    position:absolute;
    top:0px;
    right:10px;
    font-size:16px;
    font-family:Verdana;
    color:#4d4d4d;
}

.dropDown{
    width:300px;
    height:30px;
    font-family:Verdana;
    font-size:15px;
}
```

To incorporate this styling information into our web pages, we need **<link>** tags and this tag should be present within the **<head>** section of a HTML document.

> **Difference between id and class in CSS?**
>
> 1. A **class** selector is a name preceded by a full stop (.) , whereas an **id** is preceded by hash sign (#).
>
> 2. An **Id** is unique and it only refers to one HTML element. But a **class** can refer to multiple elements.

Let's create a simple *Log In* page (*logIn.html*), which will contain two input fields, one for *username* and one for *password* and a submit button. For CSS information, we will be using the External CSS file *foodDeliveryCss.css*.

Before we start coding for our *Log In* page, let's look into some HTML **input** syntaxes.

The **<input>** syntax which will take only text value is:

<input type = "text"   placeholder = "*default_name* "   name = "*name*"   id = "*id*">

The **<input>** syntax which will take only password value is:

<input type = "password"   placeholder = "*default_name* "   name = "*name*"   id = "*id*">

The **<input>** syntax for submit button:

`<input type = "submit" name = `*"name"*`>`

The `<input>` syntax for radio button:

`<input type = "radio" name = "`*name*`">`

logIn.html

```html
<style>
td{
padding:20px;
}

</style>
</head>
<body>

<div class = "container">

<table>
<tr>
<a class = "backLink" href = "file:///_____/index.html">BACK</a>
</tr>

<tr>
<td><label for="uname">Username</label></td>
<td><input id = "uname" class = "fieldStyle" type = "text"
placeholder = "Enter Username" name = "username"></td>
</tr>


<tr>
<td><label for="pwd">Password</label></td>
<td><input id = "pwd" class = "fieldStyle" type = "password"
placeholder = "Enter password" name = "password"></td>
</tr>

<tr><input class = "submitButton" type = "submit"
name = "submit"></tr>
</table>

</div>

</body>
</html>
```

To incorporate the styling information from **External CSS** file *foodDelivaryCss.css* into our *logIn.html* file, we need **<link>** tags and this tag should be present within the **<head>** section of a HTML document.

```html
<!DOCTYPE html>
<html>
<head>
<title>Log In - Tasty Home Food Delivery Service</title>
<link rel="stylesheet" href="foodDelivaryCss.css">
<style>
td{
padding:20px;
}
</style>
</head>
<body>
```

From the above HTML code, you will notice few things and they are as follows:

1. The input fields are present within **<div>** container which belongs to CSS **class** *container* and its styling information is present in the **External CSS** file *foodDelivaryCss.css (please refer to the CSS code above)*.

Please Note: In order to align the **<div>** container to the center of the page, the **margin-left** and **margin-right** property should be set to **auto**.

margin - left : auto;

margin - right : auto;

29

2. The input fields are present within a table structure.

Syntax for creating a table is:

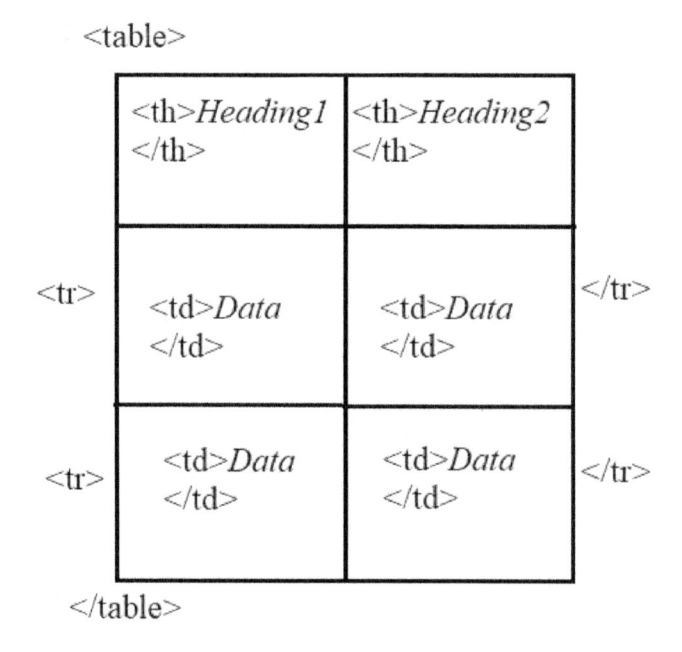

<table>

<th>…</th>

<th>.. </th>

<tr>…<td> ..</td> ..</tr>

<tr>..<td>….</td>..</tr>

……

</table>

<table>

<th>*Heading1*</th>	<th>*Heading2*</th>
<td>*Data*</td>	<td>*Data*</td>
<td>*Data*</td>	<td>*Data*</td>

(rows wrapped with <tr> ... </tr>)

</table>

<th> stands for table header
<tr> stands for table row
<td> stands for table data.

3. In the above HTML code, you will also notice the presence of <label> tag.

What is <label> tag?

<label> tag adds a meaningful user friendly text that can be associated with the html text.

This tag makes the cursor appear automatically in the input field when a user clicks on the text or some area around the text.

To connect <label> tag with its corresponding <input> tag, the input field's **id** must match with the **for** attribute of <label> tag

---

4. The input fields belongs to CSS **class** *fieldStyle*, whose styling information is present in **External CSS** file *foodDelivaryCss.css* (*please refer to CSS code above*).

5. The submit button belongs to **class** *submitButton*, whose styling information is present in the **External CSS** file *foodDelivaryCss.css*.

Now let's save everything and open *logIn.html* with Google Chrome.

All the styling information from **External CSS** file was incorporated successfully and the ***Log In*** page looks perfect.

Now let's discuss about few other important HTML tags which are used often while creating a web page.

- **<p>** tag

    <p> stands for paragraph and it mainly used to write block of text within it.

- **<select>** tag

    This tag is used to create a drop down menu.

The syntax is:

```
<select>
<option value = " val1 "> Name_1 </option>
<option value = " val2 "> Name_2 </option>
......
</select>
```

- **<form> tag**

The **<form>** tag is used to create an HTML **form** where a user can enter data.

The most important attribute of a **<form>** tag is its **action** attribute. The action attribute contains a **url** and once the **form** is submitted, the **form** data gets send to that specified **url**.

The syntax is:

```
<form action = "url_name" method = "post">
....
</form>
```

The two important **form** methods to process data from one page to another are: **GET** and **POST**

<u>**GET**</u> – This methods appends **form** data into the URL name. This makes the entire process risky because if a user sends confidential information, it will appear on the URL.

<u>**POST**</u> – This method appends **form** data with the HTTP request and not with the URL.

1.2.3: In-Line CSS

Few important points to note in In-Line CSS are:

In In-Line CSS, the styling information is added with the HTML element by using the **style** attribute. Example:
<h1 style = "*font-family : Verdana;*"> *Hello World* </h1>

Developers usually avoid In-line CSS because:

1. It makes the HTML code look messy and big. The best practice is to separate the content and the design portion.

2. As our HTML document starts to become big and complex, In-line CSS becomes confusing and harder to maintain.

3. It is time consuming.

Chapter 2: Introduction to Python Programming.

Python is the most popular and most widely used **scripting language**. Its syntax is easy to use and is written to make coding easy.

2.1: Python Installation

Step 1: Go to https://www.python.org/downloads/ and download the latest Python version available.

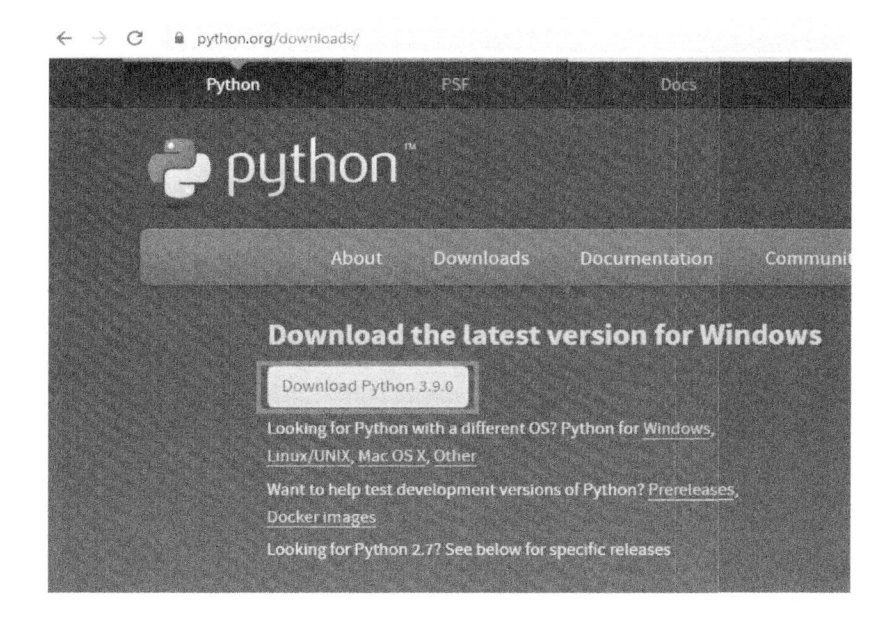

Step 2: Click on Customize installation.

For your Python download, it is important to give your own desirable path location which is short and easy to remember. This is because we will be using this path location again for **Selenium installation**.

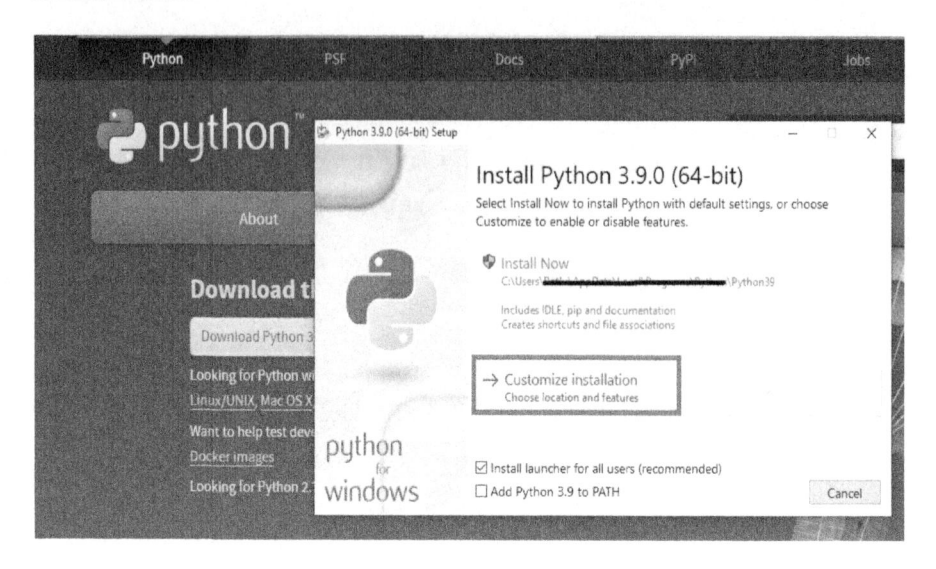

Step 3: Click Next

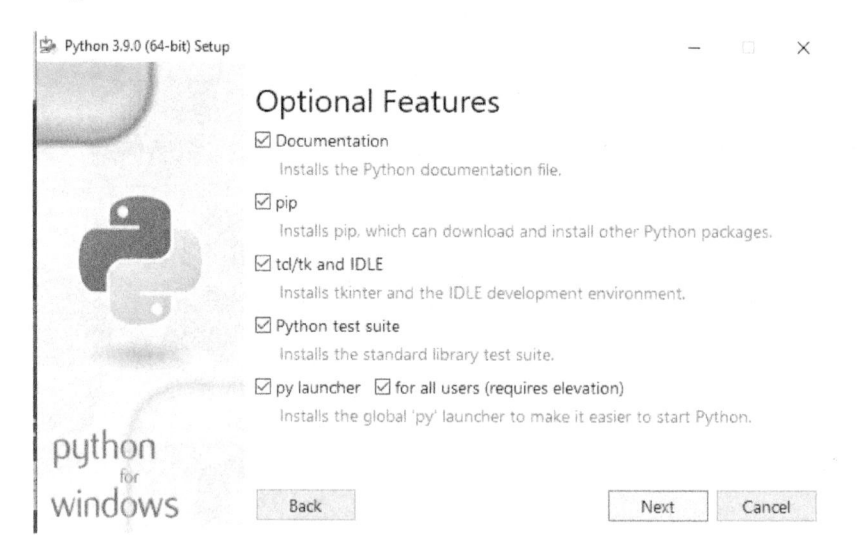

Step 4: Then browse for your install location.

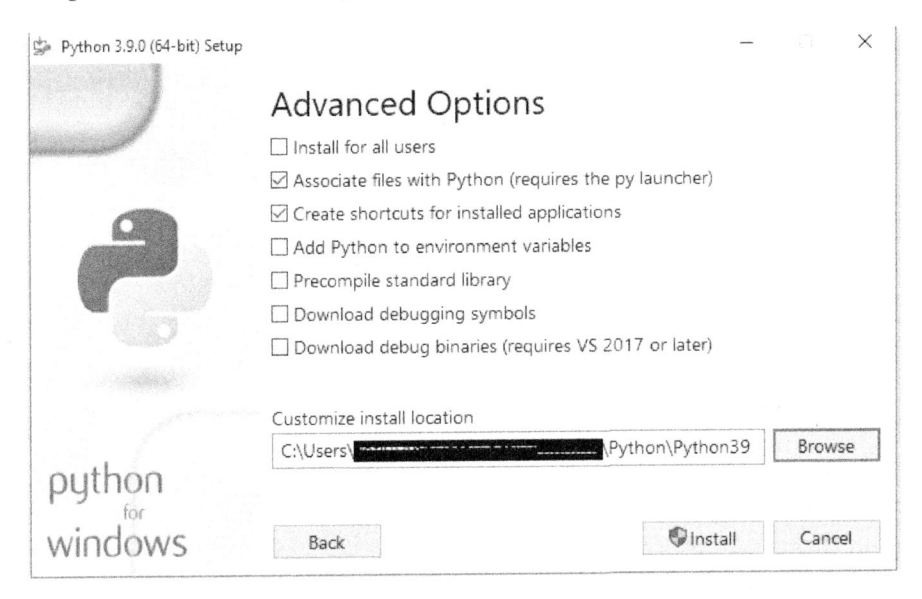

Step 5: Click install

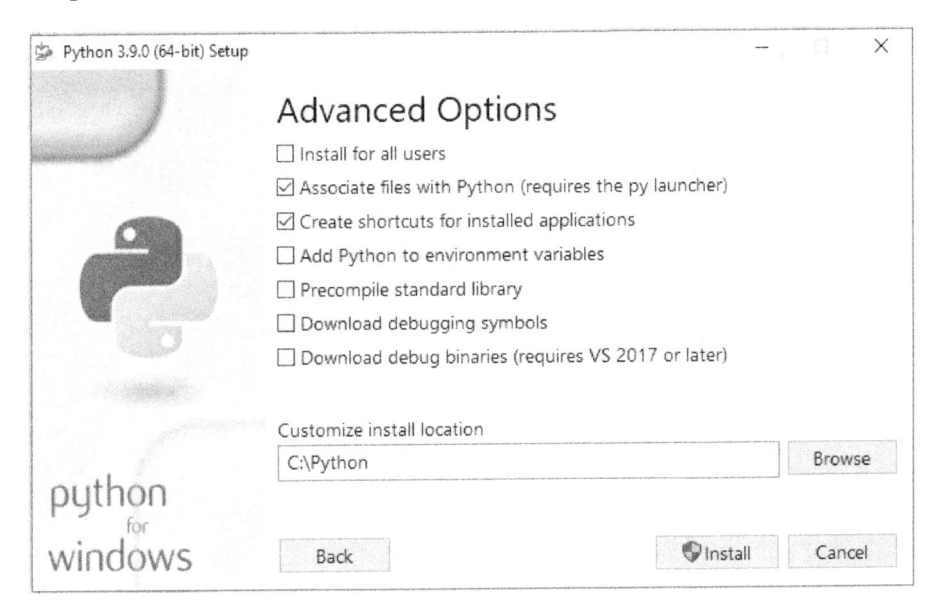

Step 6: Now go to **Control panel -> System and Security -> System -> Advanced system settings -> Environment Variables** -> Add Python Installation location into your PATH variables.

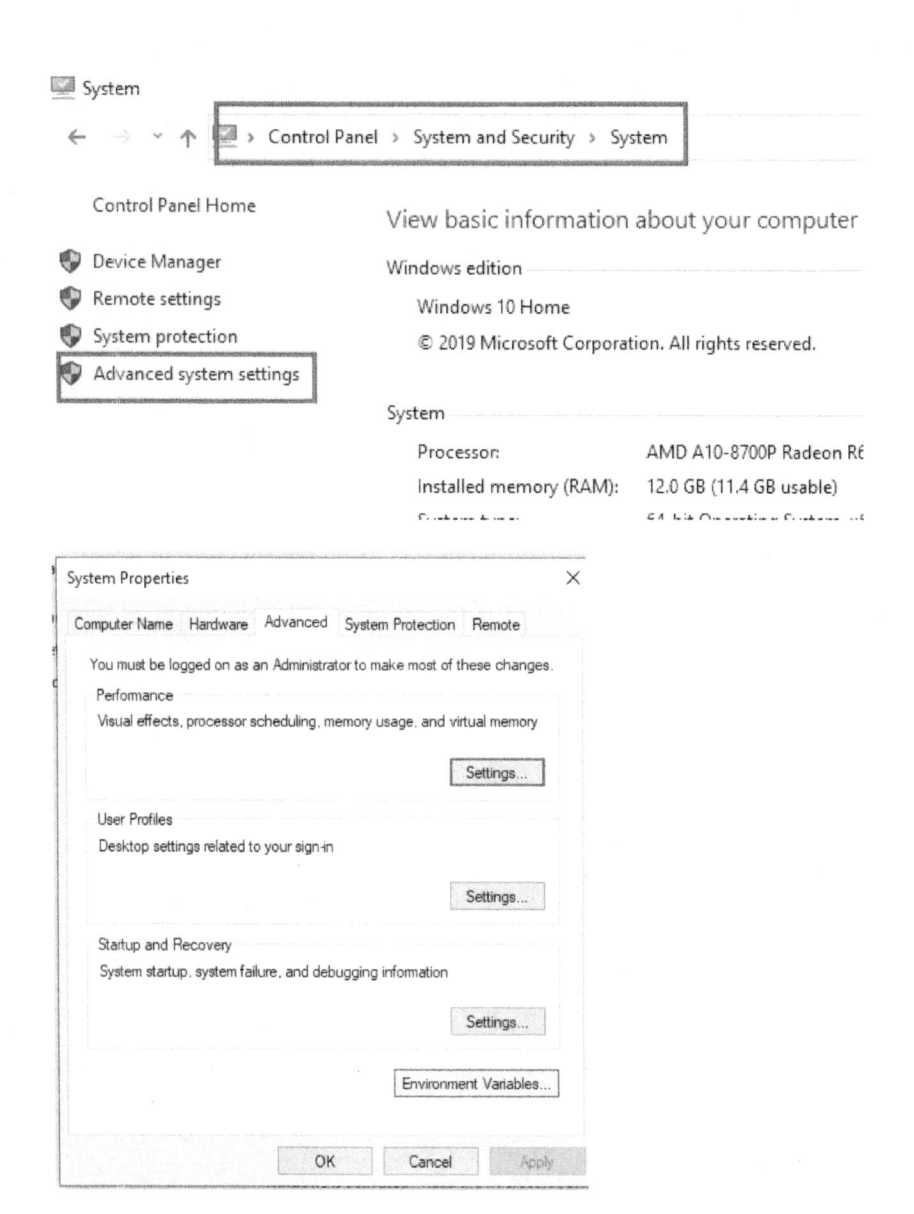

Step 7: Open command prompt and with the help of **python** command check whether installation is done correctly or not.

```
C:\>python
Python 3.9.0 (tags/v3.9.0:9cf6752, Oct  5 2020, 15:34:40) [MSC v.1927 64 bit (AMD64)] on win32
Type "help", "copyright", "credits" or "license" for more information.
>>>
```

Now let's code..

Open **Notepad++** and create a new file (*hello_world*) and save the file with **.py** extension

File name:	hello_world
Save as type:	Python file (*.py;*.pyw)

Pascal source file (*.pas;*.pp;*.p;*.inc;*.lpr)
Perl source file (*.pl;*.pm;*.plx)
PHP Hypertext Preprocessor file (*.php;*.php3;*.php4;*.php5;*.phps;*.phpt;*.phtml)
PostScript file (*.ps)
Windows PowerShell (*.ps1;*.psm1)
Properties file (*.properties)
PureBasic file (*.pb)
Python file (*.py;*.pyw)
R programming language (*.r;*.s;*.splus)
REBOL file (*.r2;*.r3;*.reb)

Inside *hello_world.py* file, write one line of code:

```
1    print("Hello World")
```

What is print( ) function in Python?
print( ) function displays the output to the screen

Now let's run the Python file.

Open command prompt -> Go the ***hello_world.py*** file location and write the following command:

python *file_name*.**py**

```
C:\>cd C:\Users\███████████\Python_script
C:\Users\███████████\Python_script>python hello_world.py
Hello World
C:\Users\███████████\Python_script>
```

2.2: Python Datatype and variables

In most programming languages, you need to declare the datatype of a variable like **int** *x* = *5*, **String** *y* = "*Hello*" etc. But in Python, you do not have to declare the data types of a variable. Python understands the datatype of any variable simply from its value. Example:

```
1    x = 5
2    y = 5.5
3    z = "Hello World"
4    print(type(x))
5    print(type(y))
6    print(type(z))
```

Output

```
C:\Users\...\Python_script>variables.py
<class 'int'>
<class 'float'>
<class 'str'>
```

What is type( ) function?

type( ) function is used to determine the data type of a variable.

When we run the above piece of code, Python shows the data types of variable *x*, *y* and *z*.

Apart from data types like **int**, **float** and **string**, Python also has **list**, **tuple** and **dictionaries**.

41

2.3: Python List

A Python **List** is very similar to an **Array**. It contains a list of elements separated by commas and its elements are written with square brackets [....].

```
1  fruits = ["apple","orange","banana","mango","strawberry","peaches"]
2  x = "this apple is tasty"
3  print(len(fruits))
4  print(fruits[2:4])
5  print(x[2:8])
```

Output

```
C:\Users\____\Desktop\Python_script>variables.py
6
['banana', 'mango']
is app
```

Code explanation:

len( ) function is used to get the length of the list.

print (fruits [2 : 4]) means print elements from position 2 (*including its value*) to position 4 (*excluding its value*).

```
            0      1       2        3         4          5
fruits = ["apple","orange","banana","mango","strawberry","peaches"]
```

42

Output: *['banana', 'mango']*

print (x [2 : 8]) means print the values of *x* ("*this apple is tasty*") from position 2 (*including its value*) to position 8 (*excluding its value*).

```
      0 1 2 34 5 6 7 8 9
x = t h i s   a p p l e   i s   t a s t y
```

Output: *is app*

2.4: Python Tuple

A **Tuple** is very much like a **List**. It contains elements separated by commas within open and close parenthesis (....).

Difference between Tuple and List

Tuple	List
Tuple contains elements within (…) parenthesis	List contains elements within […] square brackets
Once a tuple is created, no item can be added, updated or deleted	List gives us the ability to add, update and delete items.

```
1  fruits = ["apple","orange","banana","mango","strawberry","peaches"]
2  car = ("toyota","ford","volvo","tesla")
3  del(fruits[1])
4  print(fruits)
5  del(car[2])
6  print(car)
```

Output

```
C:\Users\...\Python_script>variables.py
['apple', 'banana', 'mango', 'strawberry', 'peaches']
Traceback (most recent call last):
  File "C:\Users\...\Desktop\Python_script\variables.py", line 5, in <module>
    del(car[2])
TypeError: 'tuple' object doesn't support item deletion
```

del ( ) function is used to delete element from a certain position. When applying delete function to *fruits* **list**, the value at position 1 (*orange*) was deleted successfully. But in case of **tuple**, when we tried to delete an element at position 2, it threw an error.

2.5: Python Dictionary

- Python dictionaries are used to store **key - value** pairs where the key should be a unique value.

- A dictionary is written within { ... } curly braces.

44

```
1   score = {
2   "John"  :  95,
3   "Rita"  :  90,
4   "Sam"   :  80
5   }
6   print("John scored", score['John'])
```

Output

```
C:\Users\...........\Python_script>variables.py
John scored 95
```

2.6: Python control statements

I am sure you all must be familiar with control statements like **if else, for loop, while loop**. The concept of control statements in Python is the same but it has some minor differences. They are:

1. The syntax is different.

2. In other programming languages, the control statements block of codes is written within curly braces { ...}, whereas in Python, indentation marks the beginning and end of a block of code.

45

```
1    car = ["toyota","ford","tesla","truck"]
2    for x in car:
3        if x == "tesla":
4            print("I wish to own tesla one day")
5        elif x == "truck":
6            print("But trucks are the best")
7        else:
8            print("I am fine with any car")
9
```

Output

```
C:\Users\           \Python_script>loops.py
I am fine with any car
I am fine with any car
I wish to own tesla one day
But trucks are the best
```

Important points to note are:

1. colon(:) marks the beginning of the block of codes.

2. After initiating the **for** loop, we gave an indentation and then started our **if** loop. That one indentation signifies that the **if** block of code belongs to the **for** loop.
   Now within **if** block of code, I gave two indentation to signify that the line *print("I wish to own tesla one day")* belongs to **if** statement which in turn belongs to the **for** loop.

We followed the same above process for **elif** and **else** block of codes.

3. Python **elif** means else if

2.7: Python functions.

Functions are block of codes performing certain task.

The syntax for declaring a function is:

def *function_name* ( ) :

....

```
1  username = "John123"
2  def validate_username(uname):
3      if uname == "John123":
4          print("Hello John")
5      else:
6          print("Wrong username")
7  validate_username(username)
```

Code Explanation:

- In the above piece of code, we created a **function** *validate_username* with parameter *uname*. If the argument is "*John123*", the **function** prints "*Hello John*" or else it will print "*Wrong username*".

- To call any function, we simply have to write the function name followed by parenthesis. Within that parenthesis, we passed the value of *username* which is "*John123*".

Output

```
C:\Users\███████████\Python_script>functions.py
Hello John
```

2.8: Python class

Python is an **object oriented programming language**.

A **class** is a "blueprint" for creating an **object** and like any other programming language Python **class** contains attributes and methods.

- The syntax for creating a class is:

    class *class_name* :

        def __init__(self) :

....

def *method1* :

....

What is def __init__ (self)?

"**__init__**" is a reserved method in **Python** classes initializing the **object**'s state. In Object Oriented concepts, it refers to the **constructor** of the **class**. This method initializes the attributes of a **class** when an **object** is created.

self keyword helps to access the attributes of the class.

```
1  class Employee:
2      def __init__(self,id_num,name,age,address,salary):
3          self.id_num  =  id_num
4          self.name  =  name
5          self.age  =  age
6          self.address  =  address
7          self.salary  =  salary
8      def validation(self):
9          if (str(self.id_num)  ==  "123"  and  self.name  =="John"):
10             print("This is Jon and his age is",self.age,
11             ",his address is",self.address,
12             "and his salary is",  self.salary)
13         else:
14             print("Not John")
15 e = Employee(123,"John",25,"Texas",1000)
16 e.validation()
```

Output

```
C:\Users\......\Python_script>classes.py
This is Jon and his age is 25 ,his address is Texas and his salary is 1000
```

Important points to note from the above piece of code are:

1. A Python **Class** name should start with a capital letter.

2. Within the __init__ method we declared different attributes of our **class** *Employee* and passed those values to *self* . *id_num*, *self. name* and so on.

50

3. In our ***validation ( )*** method we pass the argument **self** which helps to access all the attributes of the **class *Employee***.

4. **str( ) function** helps to convert an integer value to a string value.

5. **and** keyword is the **logical and operator** in Python.

6. In line 15 of our above code, we declared an **object *e*** and passed values into it.

2.9: Python Inheritance

Python Inheritance is very much like Java Inheritance where a class (**Child Class**) inherits all properties and methods from a base class (**Parent class**).

Benefits of Inheritance are:

1. Helps in code reusability.
2. Prevent repetitive work or code duplication.
3. Saves time.

The syntax is**:**

Class Parent:

      ……….

Class Child (Parent):

....

```python
class Employee:
    def __init__(self, c_id, c_name):
        self.c_id = c_id
        self.c_name = c_name
    def comp_info(self):
        print("The Comp id is ", self.c_id)
        print("The comp name is ", self.c_name)

class Tester(Employee):
    def __init__(self,c_id,c_name,e_id,department):
        #------INVOKING THE __INIT__ METHOD OF PARENT CLASS-----#
        Employee.__init__(self,c_id,c_name)
        self.e_id = e_id
        self.department = department
    def tester_info(self):
        print("The qa_tester's id is ",self.e_id)
        print("The qa_tester's department is ",self.department)

e = Tester(12345,"Amazon",5,"QA Automation")
e.comp_info()
e.tester_info()
```

Code explanation:

- In above piece of code, *Employee* is the **super class** and it contains attributes *c_id* and *c_name*. It also contains a **function** *comp_info* which prints out the *c_id* and *c_name*.

  Employee **super class** can be divided into many **sub classes** like *employees belonging to Testing department, employees belonging to Development department* or *customer service department* and so on.
  For now we will create only one **child class (*Tester*)** of **super class *Employee*.**

- *Tester* is the **child class** of *Employee* and it contains some standard attributes like *company_id (c_id), company_name (c_name), employee_id (e_id), department_name (department)*.

  The **class *Tester*** inherits the *c_id* and *c_name* from its **super class** and in order to make the Inheritance work properly, **we need to invoke the __init__ method of its parent class** as shown in the screen shot above. If we do not invoke, then we will get exceptions as shown in the screen shot below:

  ```
  AttributeError: 'Tester' object has no attribute 'c_id'
  ```

- **Function *tester_info* of class *Tester*,** prints out *e_id* and *department*.

- **Object *e*** is created for **class *Tester*** and all the arguments are passed into it.

Then the **function** *comp_info( )* from **super class** *Employee* and *tester_info ( )* from **child class** *Tester* is called.

Output

```
C:\Users\...\Desktop\Python_script\selenium\selenium_project>python inheri.py
The Comp id is  12345
The comp name is  Amazon
The qa_tester's id is  5
The qa_tester's department is  QA Automation
```

2.10: Python Try Except Block

The concept of Python Try Except is very similar to Java Try Catch.

The **try** block tests certain piece of code. If that piece of code throws an exception, then that exception is caught and handled by **except** block.

finally block of code always executes at the end. This block usually contains codes like exit out of an application or closes a file etc.

The syntax is:

try:

　　........

except:

　　.........

finally:

```
try:
    x = 3
    y = "error"
    z = x/y
    print("The value of z is ",z)
except SyntaxError:
    print("received an syntax error")
except TypeError:
    print("received type error")
finally:
    print("This is python try except example")
```

Code explanation:

In the above piece of code, I passed an **integer** value to variable *x* and a **string** value to variable *y*. For this **try except** example, I purposely performed a wrong arithmetic operation between the two variables and passed that value to *z*.

We know the **try** block of code will throw an exception for sure. It can throw a **SyntaxError** or **TypeError** and these types of exceptions will be handled by their respective **except** block of code.

If the **try** block throws **SyntaxError**, then the **SyntaxError except** block will run.

If the **try** block throws **TypeError**, then the **TypeError except** block will run.

Output

```
C:\Users\█████\Desktop\Python_script\selenium\selenium_project>python try_except_example.py
received type error
This is python try except example
```

> **Please note:** In this chapter, I have covered only few important Python topics essential for coding scripts in Selenium. To gain in-depth and through knowledge of all Python topics, please visit website https://www.w3schools.com/

Chapter 3: Selenium

- Selenium is an automation testing tool used for testing web applications.

  The tests are performed by test scripts and these scripts are usually coded in popular programming languages like **Java** or **Python**.

- Selenium is a collection of different tools and among them the most important one is **Selenium Webdriver**.

What is Selenium Webdriver?

- Selenium Webdriver is an API (Application Programming Interface) that provides many inbuilt operations useful in automation like clicking a button, sending keys to an input field, getting text value from a web page and many more.

- An Automation programmer can simply **import webdriver** into his/her script and can instantly get access to all its important **classes** and **methods** useful for automating a web application.

```
from selenium import webdriver
```

3.1: Selenium Webdriver Architecture

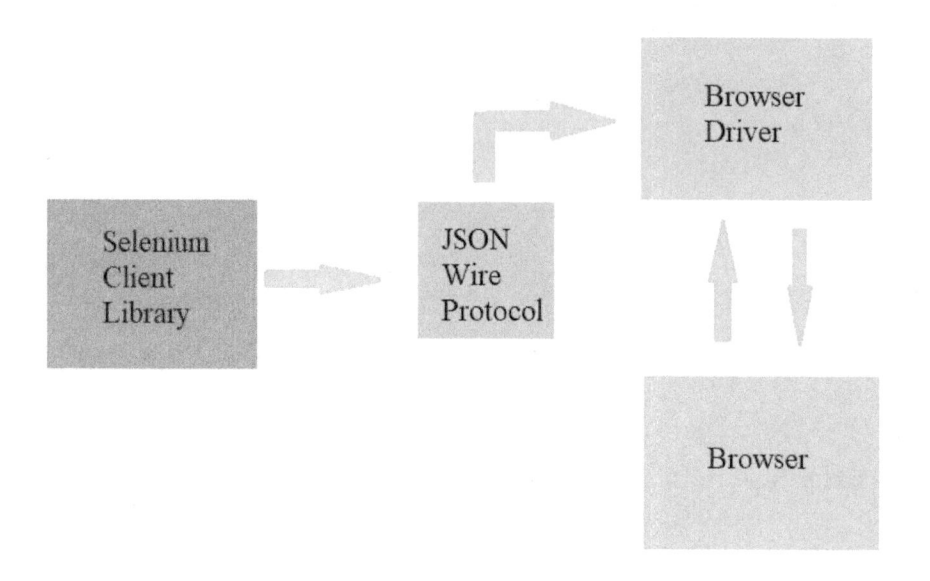

```
┌──────────┐      ┌──────────┐      ┌──────────┐
│ Selenium │      │  JSON    │      │ Browser  │
│ Client   │ ───▶ │  Wire    │      │ Driver   │
│ Library  │      │ Protocol │      │          │
└──────────┘      └──────────┘      └──────────┘
                                          ⇅
                                    ┌──────────┐
                                    │ Browser  │
                                    └──────────┘
```

- **Selenium Client Library** consists of libraries like **Python**, **Java** which is used to code Selenium scripts.

- **JSON** stands for **Javascript Object Notation** and **JSON Wire Protocol** is a **REST API** which helps to communicate between the Client and the Server.

Each **Browser Driver** has its own **HTTP Server** and **JSON Wire Protocol**'s main task is to transfer data (HTTP request) from the Client to Server.

- **Browser Driver** takes the HTTP request and triggers the commands in its respective **Browser**.

The **Browser** then generates the HTTP response and sends it back to its respective **Drivers**

Please note: Each **Browser** has its own **Browser Driver**. For example: Google Chrome has its own browser driver, Firefox has its own browser driver etc.

Before selecting the browser for your automation testing, it is very important to install its **driver** first.

In this book we will be using **Google Chrome browser**, so we have to install **Chrome Driver** for it.

3.2: Selenium and Driver Installation

Step 1: Open command prompt -> navigate to the file location where **Python** is installed (*Python installed in Chapter 2, section 2.1*) -> Go to **Scripts** folder -> Type the following command

pip install selenium

(My Python folder is present in C drive.

C drive -> Python folder -> Script.)

```
C:\Python\Scripts>pip install selenium
Collecting selenium
  Downloading selenium-3.141.0-py2.py3-none-any.whl (904 kB)
     |████████████████████████████████| 904 kB 504 kB/s
Collecting urllib3
  Downloading urllib3-1.26.2-py2.py3-none-any.whl (136 kB)
     |████████████████████████████████| 136 kB 3.3 MB/s
Installing collected packages: urllib3, selenium
Successfully installed selenium-3.141.0 urllib3-1.26.2
WARNING: You are using pip version 20.2.3; however, version 20.3.1 is available.
You should consider upgrading via the 'c:\python\python.exe -m pip install --upg

C:\Python\Scripts>
```

Selenium installed successfully.

Step 2: Selenium requires **Drivers** to interact with a specific **Browser**. Since we will be using **Google Chrome browser** for automation testing, we need to download **Chrome Driver**.

Go to site https://chromedriver.chromium.org/downloads and download the latest **Chrome Driver** -> save the file in a location which is short and easy to remember.

(I saved the Chrome Driver in C driver -> in folder ChromeDriver as shown in the screen shot below)

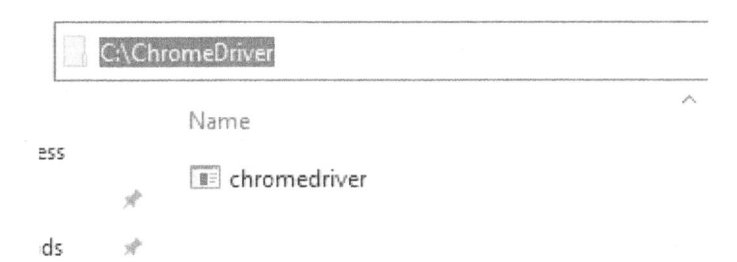

C:\ChromeDriver

Name

chromedriver

60

Now add this **Chrome Driver** location in **Environment Variables PATH** (Control panel -> System and Security -> System -> Advanced system settings -> Environment Variables).

Now let's code our first Selenium Test Script

Example 1

In this example, Let's open www.google.com through Selenium code.

> **Please note:** We will be using **Notepad++** to write all our selenium codes.

Open **Notepad++** -> create a new **python** file (*I named my file hello_world.py*)

File name:	hello_world
Save as type:	Python file (*.py;*.pyw)

Folders

In *hello_world.py* file write the following lines of code.

```
1   from selenium import webdriver
2   driver = webdriver.Chrome()
3   driver.maximize_window()
4   driver.get("https://www.google.com/")
```

Code explanation:

Line 1: importing **webdriver API** from **selenium**.

Line 2: the instance of **Chrome Driver** is created.

Line 3: accessing the **maximize_window( )** method.

maximize_window( ) method simply maximizes the window.

Line 4: with the help of **get( )** method, the specified URL opens in a new window.

Now let's save everything and run the **python** code.

Open command prompt -> navigate to the *hello_world.py* file location -> type the following command:

python *hello_world.py*

```
C:\Users\     \Desktop\Python_script\selenium\selenium_project>python hello_world.py
```

Our first selenium script ran successfully.

3.3: Locating Web Page Elements

In automation testing, all the components of a web page should be tested. To test each individual component, the first thing which we need to do is to locate them with the help of their **ID** or **class name** or **tag name** etc.

We have discussed about HTML element's **ID** and **class name** in chapter 1. Now in this section, we will discuss about how to access these essential information from a web page.

Step 1: Open the *Tasty Food Delivery Service* website which we created in chapter 1

Link: http://sbasu.pythonanywhere.com/tastyFoodApp/

(This web site is created for automation practice purpose only)

On the *Create New Profile* link, **right click** -> then click on **Inspect**

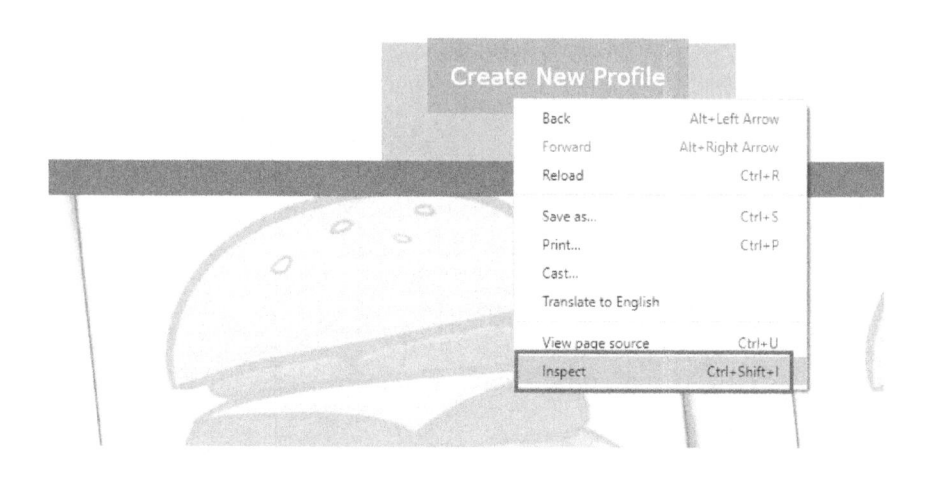

The HTML information about that web element appears.

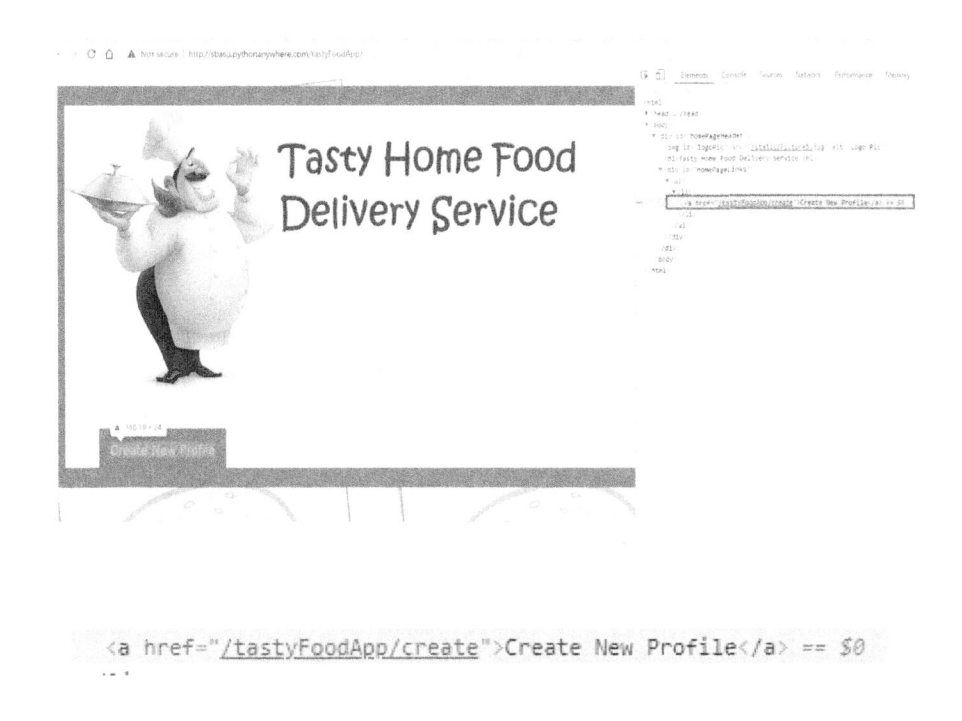

```
<a href="/tastyFoodApp/create">Create New Profile</a> == $0
```

Step 2: Now examine the above piece of HTML code.

The code above does not contain any **ID** or **class name**, so how we can locate and access this web element from our test script ?.

We can access this **Link** web element with the help of **find_element_by_link_text** (*link_name*) method provided by **selenium webdriver.**

Let's inspect another web element.

Proceed to the *Create New Profile* page (Link: http://sbasu.pythonanywhere.com/tastyFoodApp/create).

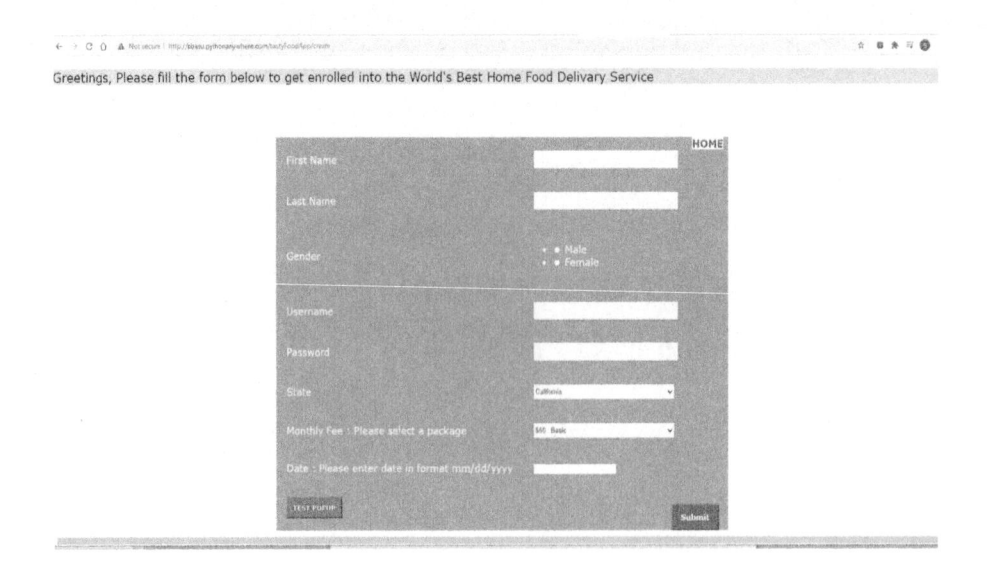

On the *First Name* **input** field, **right click -> Inspect**

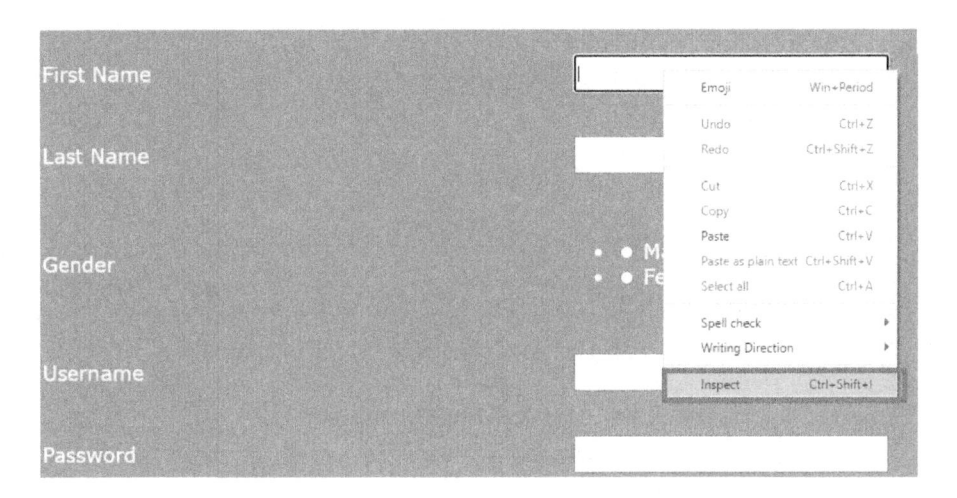

The HTML information about that web element appears.

```
▼<table>
    ▼<tbody>
        <tr>
        </tr>
    ▼<tr>
        ▶<td>…</td>
            <input type="text" name="firstName" class="fieldStyle"
            required id="id_firstName"> == $0
        </td>
    </tr>
    ▶<tr>…</tr>
```

Now examine the highlighted code above. You will notice that the *First Name* **input** field has an **ID** *id_firstName*. With the help of this information along with **selenium webdriver** method **find_element_by_id** (*id_name*) we can locate this element from *Create New Profile* page.

So by following the above process we can get critical information about a web page element. This information along with **selenium webdriver** methods help in automation.

NOTE: ID should be the first priority to find web elements.

Most important and commonly used webdriver methods for locating a web element are:

find_element_by_id (*id_name*)

find_element_by_name (*name*)

67

find_element_by_xpath (*xpath*)

find_element_by_link_text (*link_name*)

find_element_by_partial_link_text (*partial_link_text_name*)

find_element_by_tag_name (*tag_name*)

find_element_by_class_name (*class_name*)

find_element_by_css_selector (*css_selector*)

Example 1

In this example, the automation script will locate the *Create New Profile* link in the *Home page* and click on it.

Step 1: Open **Notepad++** -> create a new **python** file and I named my file *testing.py*.

In *testing.py* file, write the following lines of code.

```
from selenium import webdriver
driver = webdriver.Chrome()
driver.maximize_window()
driver.get("http://sbasu.pythonanywhere.com/tastyFoodApp/")
```

(code explanation present in section 3.2 -> Example 1)

Step 2: Open *Home page* (http://sbasu.pythonanywhere.com/tastyFoodApp/) -> **right click** on the *Create New Profile* link -> **Inspect**.

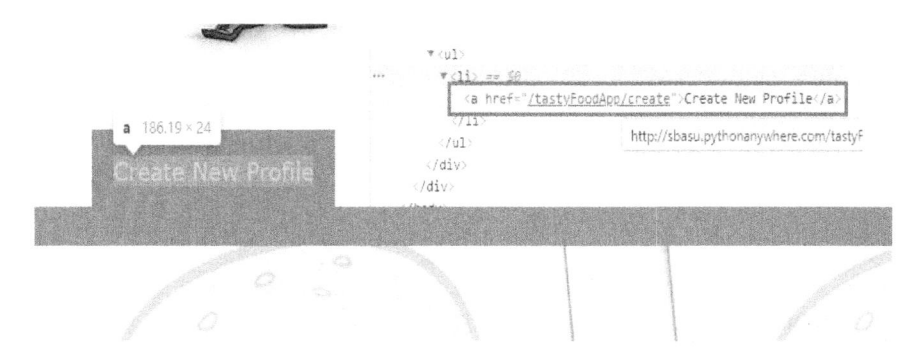

Copy the "*Create New Profile*" **link text** from the HTML code.

Step 3: Go back to **python** file *testing.py* and write the highlighted lines of code shown below.

```python
from selenium import webdriver
driver = webdriver.Chrome()
driver.maximize_window()
driver.get("http://sbasu.pythonanywhere.com/tastyFoodApp/")
element = driver.find_element_by_link_text("Create New Profile")
element.click()
```

Code explanation:

- We passed the *Create New Profile* **link text** copied in Step 2 into **find_element_by_link_text ( )** method

69

- Line *element = driver.find_element_by_link_text("Create New Profile")* locates the **link** and stores that HTML element within a variable *element*.

- With the help of **click( )** method we clicked on the element.

Now let's save everything and run our script.

Open command prompt -> navigate to the *testing.py* file location -> with **python** command run the script.

```
C:\Users\▓▓▓▓\Desktop\Python_script\test>python testing.py
```

Our script runs successfully.

Example 2

In this example, we will enter some text values within the input fields and click on a radio button.

Open *Create New Profile* page, **right click** on the *First Name* input field -> **Inspect**.

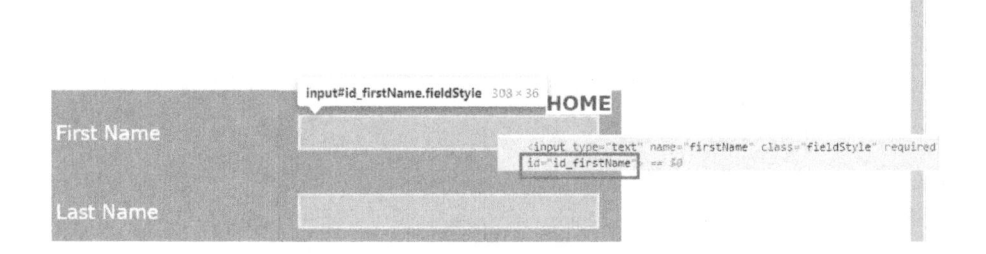

The ***First Name* input field** has an **ID** *id_firstName*.

Like this you will notice that all the input fields and the radio buttons of *Create New Profile* page have an **ID**. This information along with **find_element_by_id( )** method will help to locate these elements.

Open our existing **python** file *testing.py* and add the following lines of code.

```
#-------First Name input field----------
firstName = driver.find_element_by_id('id_firstName')
firstName.send_keys("Kia")
#--------Last Name input field----------
lastName = driver.find_element_by_id('id_lastName')
lastName.send_keys("Taco")
#--------Radio Button-----------------
driver.find_element_by_id('id_gender_1').click()
#--------Username input field---------------
username = driver.find_element_by_id('id_username')
username.send_keys("KiaTaco")
#---------Password input field---------------
password = driver.find_element_by_id('id_password')
password.send_keys("Kia23")
```

Code explanation:

In the above piece of code, we are simply locating the web elements and storing them in their respective variables.

send_keys( ) method is used to send some values within those input fields.

Let's save everything and run the script with the help of **python** command.

```
C:\Users\███████\Desktop\Python_script\test>python testing.py
```

Our script runs successfully.

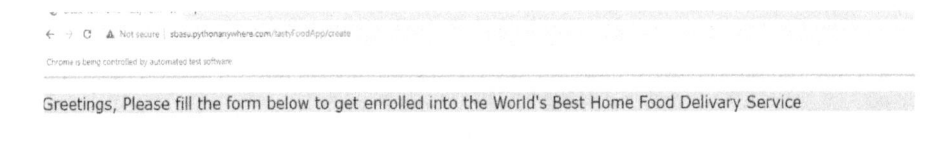

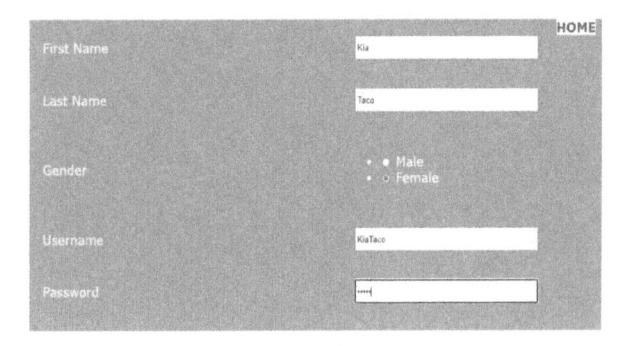

Greetings, Please fill the form below to get enrolled into the World's Best Home Food Delivery Service

		HOME
First Name	Kia	
Last Name	Taco	
Gender	● Male ○ Female	
Username	KiaTaco	
Password	••••	

Please note: If you face any difficulty while running the script (*testing.py*), please add the highlighted line of code shown in the screen shot below.

```
time.sleep(10)
```
```
#-------First Name input field------
firstName  =  driver.find_element_by_
firstName.send_keys("Kia")
val1  =  firstName.get_attribute('va
print("The first name is", val1)
#--------Last Name input field------
lastName  =  driver.find_element_by_
```

Add this line just before filling out the *Create New Profile* **form** page and this will tell **selenium webdriver** to pause execution for 10 seconds before working with *Create New Profile page* from *Home page*.

Please do not forget to **Import time module** before using this method.

```
import  time
```

Example 3

In this example, we will select a value from the drop down menu.

To work with drop down menus **selenium webdriver** provides us with **Select class**.

73

> **The most important methods present in Select class are:**
>
> **select_by_visible_text ( )** – This method is used to select an option value by visible text
>
> **select_by_index( )** – This method is used to select an option value by index number
>
> **select_by_value( )** – This method is very similar to the above two methods, where it selects an option based on the value provided to the method.
>
> **deselect_all( )** - This method is used to deselect all selected option values.

Now open *testing.py* file and add the following lines of code.

```python
#----------select state-------------------
state = Select(driver.find_element_by_id('id_state'))
state.select_by_visible_text('Texas')
#----------select fee --------------------
fee = Select(driver.find_element_by_id('id_fee'))
fee.select_by_visible_text('$150 : Gold')
```

Please note: To work with **selenium webdriver Select class**, we need to **import** it first.

```
from selenium import webdriver
from selenium.webdriver.support.ui import Select

driver = webdriver.Chrome()
driver.maximize_window()
driver.get("http://sbasu.pythonanywhere.com/tastyFoo
element = driver.find_element_by_link_text("Create
element.click()
#-------First Name input field----------
firstName = driver.find_element_by_id('id_firstNam
```

Now let's save everything and run our script.

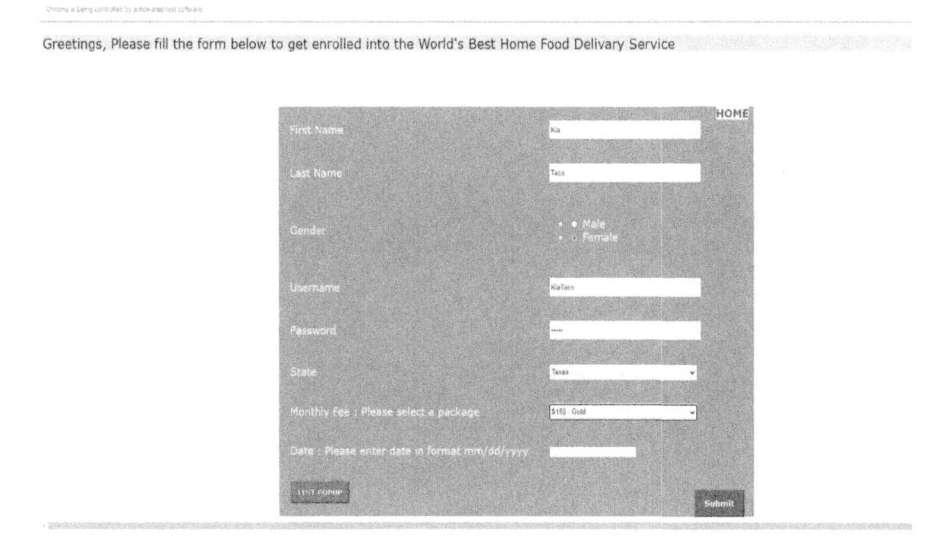

Our script ran successfully.

Example 4

In this example, we will deal with any alert window present in our web page.

Open *Create New Profile* page -> On *TEST POPUP* button, **right click -> Inspect**.

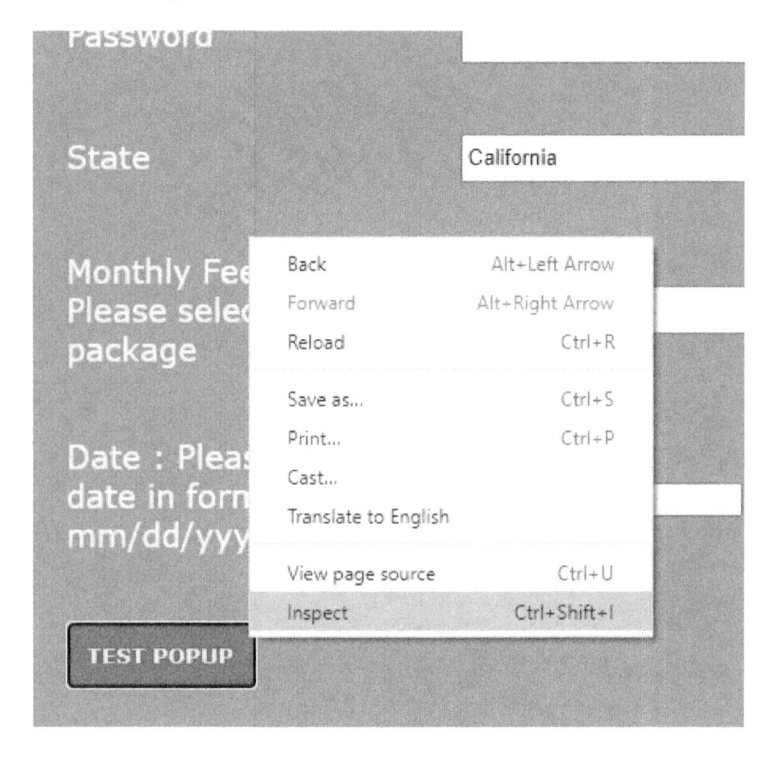

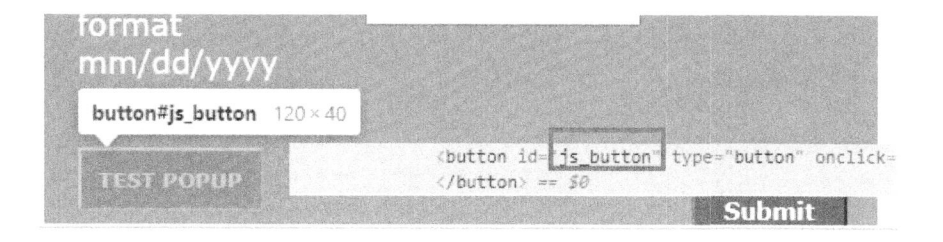

The button has an **ID** *js_button*. With the help of this information and along with **selenium webdriver** method **find_element_by_id( )** we can click on it.

Open our existing *testing.py* file and add the following lines of code.

```
#-----------alert window--------------------
button = driver.find_element_by_id('js_button')
print("Is Button enabled",button.is_enabled())
button.click()
alert = driver.switch_to_alert()
alert.accept()
```

Code explanation:

- o **is_enabled( )** method checks whether the web element in enabled or not and it returns a Boolean value.

- **switch_to_alert( )** method switches focus to an alert window.

- **accept( )** method is used to click on OK button of alert window.

Now let's save everything and run our script.

Open command prompt -> navigate to *testing.py* file location -> run using **python** command.

```
C:\Users\     \Desktop\Python_script\test>python testing.py
DevTools listening on ws://127.0.0.1:57278/devtools/browser/
[10568:4256:1208/125409.160:ERROR:device_event_log_impl.cc(2
d to read descriptor from node connection: A device attached
[10568:4256:1208/125409.176:ERROR:device_event_log_impl.cc(2
73 Getting Default Adapter failed.
The first name is Kia
Is Button enabled True
C:\Users\     \Desktop\Python_script\test\testing.py:36: Dep
  alert = driver.switch_to_alert()
The text matches
```

Our script runs successfully and we also get the Boolean output stating that the button was enabled.

Example 5

In this example, we would like to test, whether the paragraph text on a web page matches with the expected value or not. If matches return TRUE, else return FALSE.

Open *Create New Profile* page, you will notice that at the top of the page a line is written highlighted in the screen shot below

![Screenshot showing a browser with URL http://sbasu.pythonanywhere.com/tastyFoodApp/create and a highlighted text box reading: "Greetings, Please fill the form below to get enrolled into the World's Best Home Food Delivery Service" followed by First Name and Last Name input fields.]

In this example, we will access this value and check whether it matches with the expected value or not.

The expected value is:

"Greetings, Please fill the form below to get enrolled into the World's Best Home Food Delivery Service"

Please Note: Automation programmers usually find the expected value from product specification document provided by the company.

Let's access the text value from the *Create New Profile* page,

Right click on the paragraph text value -> **Inspect**.

[Screenshot showing HTML inspector with paragraph element of class "text" containing "Greetings, Please fill the form below to get enrolled into the World's Best Home Food Delivery Service", and a Last Name form field]

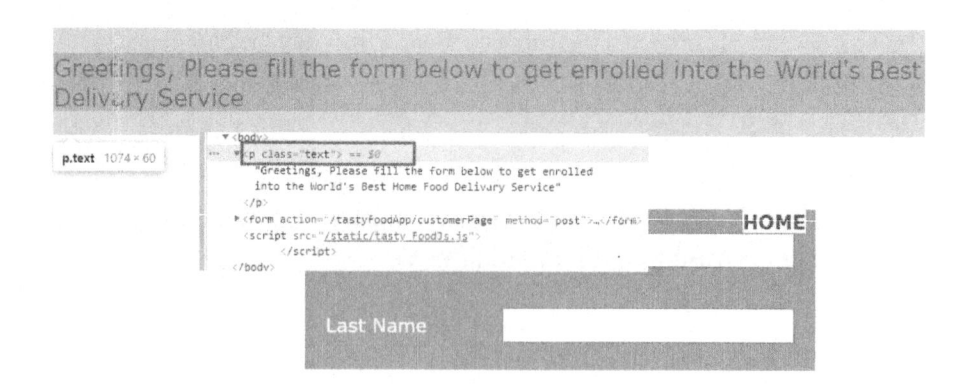

You will notice that the paragraph field belongs to **class *text***. Since there is no other element in the ***Create New Profile*** page using this same **class name,** so we will be using this attribute along with **selenium webdriver find_element_by_class_name( )** method to uniquely identify the web element.

Open ***testing.py*** file and add the following lines of code:

```python
#---------------testing text---------------
received_intro = driver.find_element_by_class_name('text').text
expected_intro = "Greetings, Please fill the form below to get enrolled into the World's Best Home Food Delivery Service"
if received_intro==expected_intro:
    print("The text matches")
else:
    print("The text does not match")
```

- **text** method helps to return the text value from a paragraph.

Now let's save everything and run our code.

Open command prompt -> navigate to the *testing.py* file location -> run the script using **python** command.

The script runs successfully and I also get the output stating that the text matches.

```
C:\Users\     \Desktop\Python_script\test>python testing.py

DevTools listening on ws://127.0.0.1:56454/devtools/browser/
[7356:4028:1208/122753.483:ERROR:device_event_log_impl.cc(2
 to read descriptor from node connection: A device attached
[7356:4028:1208/122753.505:ERROR:device_event_log_impl.cc(2
3 Getting Default Adapter failed.
Is Button enabled True
C:\Users\    \Desktop\Python_script\test\testing.py:34: De
  alert = driver.switch_to_alert()
The text matches
```

Example 6

In this example, we would like to GET the value from the *First Name* input field.

In *testing.py* file, add the following lines of code

```
#--------First Name input field-----------
firstName = driver.find_element_by_id('id_firstName')
firstName.send_keys("Kia")
val1 = firstName.get_attribute('value')
print("The first name is", val1)
```

Code explanation:

- As you may recall we passed a value "*Kia*" to the **First Name** input field in **Example 2**.

    To attain that value from the input field, we used **get_attribute('value')** method and stored that value in a variable *val1*.

Now let's save everything and run our script.

The script runs successfully and we also get the *first name* as output.

```
C:\Users\____\Desktop\Python_script\test>python testing.py
DevTools listening on ws://127.0.0.1:57278/devtools/browser/33a
[10568:4256:1208/125409.160:ERROR:device_event_log_impl.cc(211)
d to read descriptor from node connection: A device attached to
[10568:4256:1208/125409.176:ERROR:device_event_log_impl.cc(211)
73 Getting Default Adapter failed.
The first name is Kia
Is Button enabled True
C:\Users\____,\Desktop\Python_script\test\testing.py:36: Deprec
  alert = driver.switch_to_alert()
The text matches
```

Example 7

In this example, we will get the URL and title of the web page and match the received title with the expected title.

Open our existing *testing.py* file and add the following lines of code.

```
#----------get url and title----------------
print("The url is ", driver.current_url)
expected_val = "Tasty Home Food Delivery Service"
received_title = driver.title
if(received_title==expected_val):
    print("The title matches")
else:
    print("The title does not match")
print("The received title is ", received_title)
```

- **driver.current_url** is used to get the URL of the web page.

- **driver.title** is used to get the title of the web page.

Now let's save everything and run our script.

Our script runs successfully.

```
C:\Users\█████\Desktop\Python_script\test>python testing.py

DevTools listening on ws://127.0.0.1:57845/devtools/browser/
[2236:2736:1208/131032.596:ERROR:device_event_log_impl.cc(21
 to read descriptor from node connection: A device attached
[2236:2736:1208/131032.617:ERROR:device_event_log_impl.cc(21
3 Getting Default Adapter failed.
The url is  http://sbasu.pythonanywhere.com/tastyFoodApp/
The title matches
The received title is  Tasty Home Food Delivery Service
The first name is Kia
Is Button enabled True
C:\Users\█ █ .\Desktop\Python_script\test\testing.py:46: Dep
  alert = driver.switch_to_alert()
The text matches
```

83

Example 8

In this example, we would like to get the highlighted text shown in the screen shot below and check whether it matches with the expected value or not.

http://sbasu.pythonanywhere.com/tastyFoodApp/create

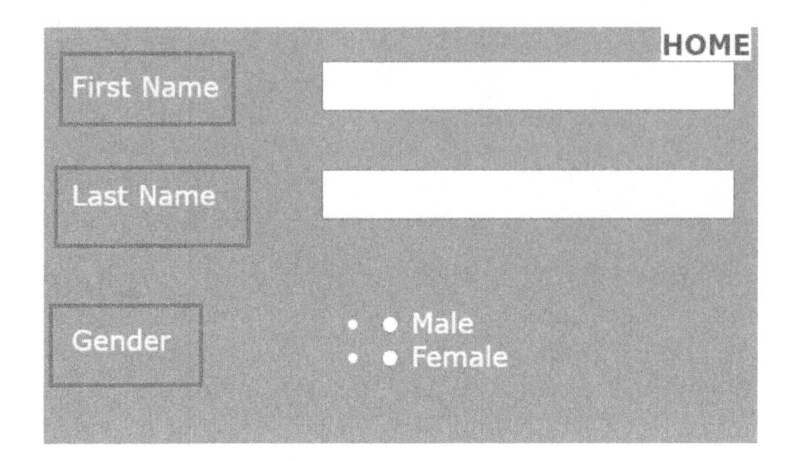

[Screenshot of Create New Profile page showing First Name, Last Name, and Gender (Male/Female) fields with HOME link]

Open *Create New Profile* page -> **right click** on the *First Name* text value -> **Inspect**

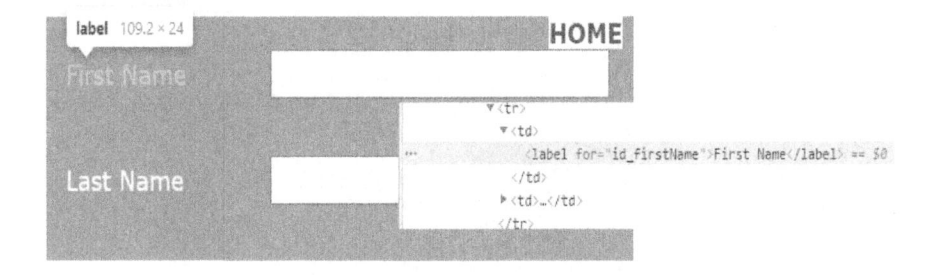

[Screenshot showing inspect element view with HTML:
```
<tr>
  <td>
    ...  <label for="id_firstName">First Name</label> == $0
  </td>
  <td>...</td>
</tr>
```
]

84

You will notice that the *First Name* text value does not contain any **ID** or **Class Name**. So in this situation how we can access the web element ?.

The answer to the question is **XPATH**.

3.3.1: XPATH

- XPATH stands for XML path.

- XPATH queries are used to locate an element from HTML DOM structure.

　　The syntax is:

// tag_name [@ attribute_name = "value"]

There are two types of XPATH:

1. Absolute XPATH
2. Relative XPATH

Absolute XPATH

Important points to note are:

- Absolute XPATH starts with a single (/) slash.

- Absolute XPATH, always starts from the root node and traverse down through all element to get to our desired element.

Example:
The screen shot below shows a *Hello World* web page.

[Hello World]

From this web page, we would like to get the *Hello World* text value and print it as output.

So let's **right click** on *Hello World* text value -> **Inspect**

```
▼<div id="parent">
  ▼<div class="child">
    ▼<table>
      ▼<tbody>
        ▼<tr>
             <td>
             Hello World
             </td> == $0
          </tr>
        </tbody>
      </table>
    </div>
  </div>
```

We see that the text value is present within: *<html>* -> *<body>* -> *<div>* *container* *ID* *"parent"* -> *<div>* *container* *class* *name* *"child"* -> *<table>* -> *<tbody>* -> *<tr>* -> *<td>* .

The Absolute XPATH will be:

/html/body/div/div/table/tbody/tr/td

Relative XPATH

Important points to note are:

- Relative XPATH starts with a double (//) slash.

- Relative XPATH does not start from the root node to get to our desired element. We can simply write a query and locate the web element using the following syntax:

    // tag_name [@ attribute_name = "value"]

87

- Relative XPATH is more preferable to use than Absolute XPATH.

The Relative XPATH of the above *Hello World* example will be:

//*[@id='parent']//td

or

//td

Example 9

In this example, we will get the value from the *Username* input field (*entered in Example 2*) and store it into a variable *entered_username*.
Once the form is submitted by clicking on the submit button, the user information gets displayed on the *Customer* web page.
We will check whether the entered username stored in variable *entered_username* matches with the displayed username (of *Customer* web page) or not.

- As you may recall in *testing.py* file, we entered a *username* in *Example 2*. Now let's get that *username* value using **get_attribute('value')** method and store it in variable *entered_username*.

```
#--------Username input field----------------
username = driver.find_element_by_id('id_username')
username.send_keys("KiaTaco")
entered_username = username.get_attribute('value')
```

- In previous *Examples* from *1* to *8*, we have filled the *Create New Profile* form with data. Now we simply have to click on the submit button.

    Open *Create New Profile* page, **right click** on Submit button -> **Inspect**.

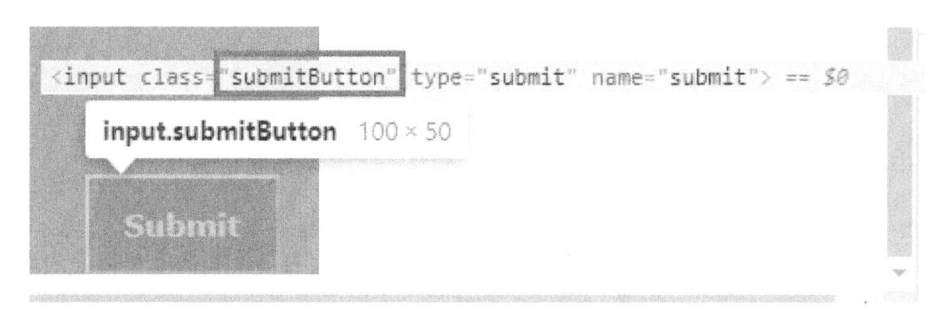

    ```
    <input class="submitButton" type="submit" name="submit"> == $0
    ```
    input.submitButton 100 × 50

    Submit

    We see that the Submit button belongs to **class** "*submitButton*". With this information along with **find_element_by_class_name( )** method, we can click on the button.

    Open *testing.py* file and add the following line of code.

89

```
#---------click on the submit button-------------
driver.find_element_by_class_name('submitButton').click()
```

- Now let's open the *customer* page. The link is: http://sbasu.pythonanywhere.com/tastyFoodApp/customerPage

| http://sbasu.pythonanywhere.com/tastyFoodApp/customerPage

Thank you..Please confirm the information below

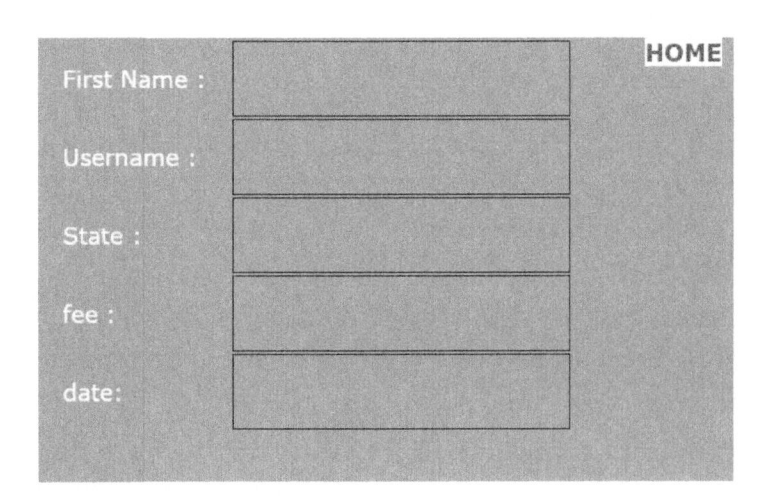

		HOME
First Name :		
Username :		
State :		
fee :		
date:		

Right click on the *Username* display field -> **Inspect**.

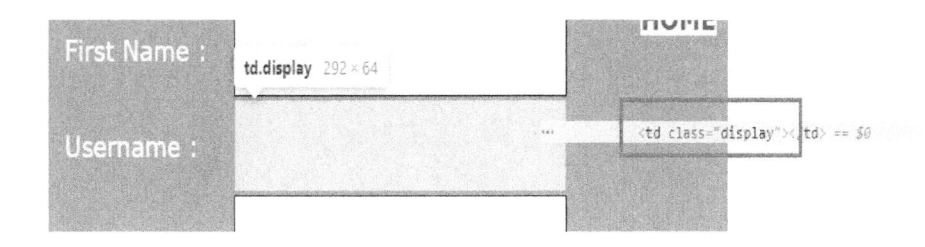

The field does not contain any unique **ID,** but it contains a **class name** *display.* It is impossible to locate this specific *Username* display field simply by its **class name** because there are many other fields in the same web page using the same **class name** as shown in the screen shot below.

So in order to uniquely identify the *Username* display field, we will be using XPATH.

To get the XPATH of a web element: **right click on the web element** (*Username* display field) -> **Inspect** -> then **right click on its HTML code** -> **Copy** -> **Copy XPATH**.

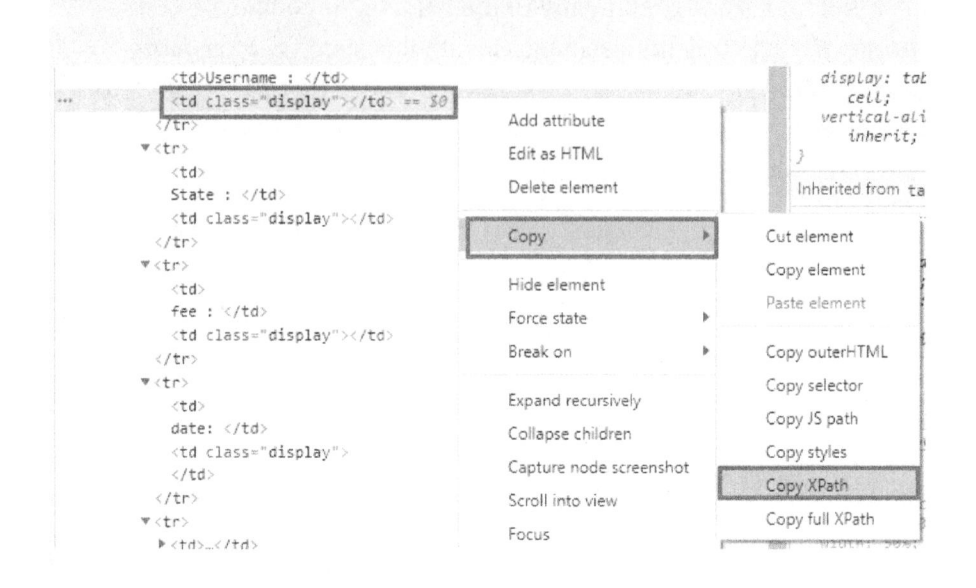

The XPATH which I received for my *Username* display field is an **Absolute XPATH** as shown by the screen shot below.

/html/body/div/table/tbody/tr[2]/td[2]

Now let's convert this **Absolute XPATH** into a **Relative** one by following the step below:

92

- Keep only the crucial information which will help to uniquely identify the *Username* display field and replace the rest with double (//) slash.

$$//tr[2]/td[2]$$

Now in *testing.py* file, add the following lines of code.

```python
displayed_username = driver.find_element_by_xpath('//tr[2]/td[2]').text
if(entered_username == displayed_username):
    print("The username matches")
else:
    print("The username does not match")
```

Code explanation:

- With the help of **text** method we receive the value from the *Username* display field of *Customer* page and store it in a variable *displayed_username*.

- Then we check whether the value stored in variable *entered_username* matches with *displayed_username* or not. If matches print "*The username matches*", else print "*The username does not match*"

Please Note: To get the value from *Username* display field of *Customer* page, we used **text** instead of **get_attribute( )** method

> because the ***Username*** display field is NOT an **input** field and **get_attribute( )** method works ONLY for **input** fields.

Let's save everything and run our script.

The script ran successfully and the ***usernames*** matched.

```
The username matches
```

3.4: Selenium Waits

For the automation testing of a web application to be successfully, the first rule we need to follow is to wait for the web page and all its elements to completely finish loading. If automation starts before the loading process, then **selenium webdriver** will not be able to locate the web elements and will throw an "**Element Not Found**" exception.

In order to prevent that from happening **selenium webdriver** provides us with two types of **waits**:

1. Implicit Wait
2. Explicit Wait

3.4.1: Implicit Wait

Implicit Wait tells **webdriver** to wait for a certain amount of time when trying to locate any web element or elements. If the element is not found within the implicit wait time then it will throw an **"Element Not Found"** exception.

The syntax is:

driver . implicitly_wait (*5*)

(where 5 is the time in **seconds**)

3.4.2: Explicit Wait

Explicit Wait tells the **webdriver** to wait for a certain condition (**Expected Conditions**) to occur before proceeding further in the code.

The syntax is:

element = **WebDriverWait (driver,** *15* **) . until (EC. visibility_of_element_located ((By.ID, "** *id_firstName* **")))**

In the above piece of code, **webdriver** waits for 15 seconds for an element with **ID** *id_firstName* to be found. If no element is found an exception is thrown.

> **NOTE:**
>
> 1. **Expected Condition** returns a Boolean value.
>
> 2. In order to work with Classes **By**, **Expected Condition** and **WebDriverWait** we need to import them.
>
> **from selenium.webdriver.common.by import By**
>
> **from selenium.webdriver.support.ui import WebDriverWait**
>
> **from selenium.webdriver.support import expected_conditions as EC**

```
from selenium import webdriver
from selenium.webdriver.common.by import By
from selenium.webdriver.support.ui import WebDriverWait
from selenium.webdriver.support import expected_conditions as EC

driver = webdriver.Chrome()
driver.maximize_window()
driver.get("http://sbasu.pythonanywhere.com/tastyFoodApp/create")

#-----Implicit Wait-------
driver.implicitly_wait(10)

#-----Explicit Wait-------
wait = WebDriverWait(driver,10)
element = wait.until(EC.presence_of_element_located((By.ID,"id_firstName")))
element.send_keys("KiaTaco")
```

Code explanation:

The above piece of code shows both Implicit Wait and Explicit Wait.

In Explicit wait, **webdriver** wait for 10 seconds for an element with **ID** *id_firstName* to be found. If the element found successfully, then value "*KiaTaco*" are send into it using **send_keys( )** method.

List of Expected Conditions that can be used in Explicit Wait

title_is

title_contains

presence_of_element_located

visibility_of_element_located

visibility_of

presence_of_all_elements_located

text_to_be_present_in_element

text_to_be_present_in_element_value

frame_to_be_available_and_switch_to_it

invisibility_of_element_located

element_to_be_clickable

staleness_of

element_to_be_selected

element_located_to_be_selected

element_selection_state_to_be

element_located_selection_state_to_be

alert_is_present

List of popular attributes available for By class

ID *(id)*

XPATH *(xpath)*

LINK_TEXT *(link text)*

PARTIAL_LINK_TEXT *(partial link text)*

NAME *(name)*

TAG_NAME *(tag name)*

CLASS_NAME *(class name)*

CSS_SELECTOR *(css selector)*

There is another way to make Selenium **webdriver** wait and that is **time.sleep(t)**, Where t is the time in seconds. Example: **time.sleep(10).** This tells **webdriver** to pause or go to sleep for 10 seconds and after 10 seconds carry on with the automation process.

In order to work with **sleep** method we need to import **time** module first.

import time

> **Please note:** Automation programmers usually avoid **sleep** method and use it only in extreme cases.

3.5: Selenium Page Object Model

Automation Developers usually design their Selenium project following the **Page Object Model framework**.

Benefits of using **Page Object Model framework** are:

1. Code reusability and removal of duplicate codes.

2. It saves time.

    If something in the web application changes, the fix needs changes only in one place.

Page Object Model Architecture

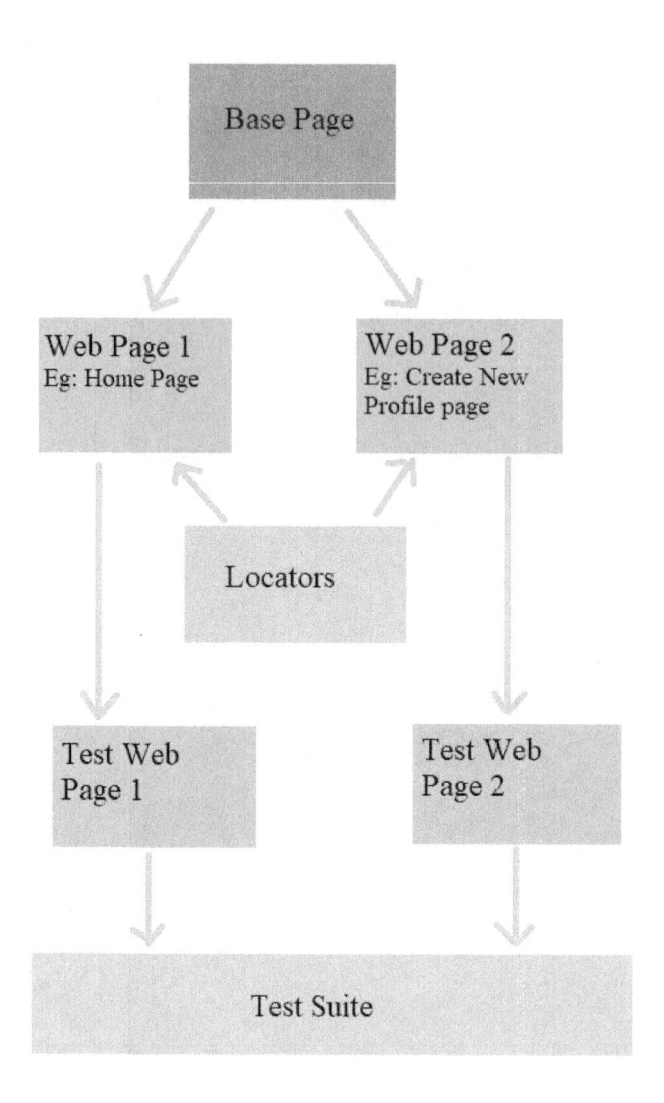

```
                    ┌─────────────┐
                    │  Base Page  │
                    └─────────────┘
                      ↙         ↘
        ┌─────────────┐         ┌─────────────┐
        │ Web Page 1  │         │ Web Page 2  │
        │ Eg: Home Page│        │ Eg: Create New│
        │             │         │ Profile page │
        └─────────────┘         └─────────────┘
              │    ↖             ↗    │
              │     ┌──────────┐      │
              │     │ Locators │      │
              │     └──────────┘      │
              ↓                       ↓
        ┌─────────────┐         ┌─────────────┐
        │  Test Web   │         │  Test Web   │
        │   Page 1    │         │   Page 2    │
        └─────────────┘         └─────────────┘
              │                       │
              ↓                       ↓
        ┌─────────────────────────────────────┐
        │            Test Suite               │
        └─────────────────────────────────────┘
```

3.5.1: Base Page

The **Base Page** is like a **Super Class**, it contains all the commonly used **methods** or **functions** which are needed often while automating a web application.

For example: accessing an input field and sending values into it, clicking on a button are some of the most commonly used task in automation testing. Instead of writing the same lines of code for these common tasks again and again, we can simply write them once (within a **function**) and store it in a place (within a **Class**).

While automating a web application, whenever we will be performing these common tasks, we can simply call its respective **function** from the **Class**.

(To understand Python function and Class please refer to Chapter 2, section 2.7 and 2.8 respectively)

So let's create a **base page** for our *Tasty Food Delivery project* http://sbasu.pythonanywhere.com/tastyFoodApp/ .

Step 1: Open **Notepad**++ -> create a new **python** file and name it *element.py*

Within *element.py* file, create a **Class** which will contain some commonly used functions.

(For demonstration purpose, I will be creating only one method).

```python
from selenium.webdriver.support.ui import WebDriverWait
from selenium.webdriver.common.by import By
from selenium.webdriver.support import expected_conditions as EC

class BasePage:
    def __init__(self,driver):
        self.driver = driver

    def set_element_id(self,locator_value,input_value):
        driver = self.driver
        element = WebDriverWait(driver,10).until(EC.presence_of_element_located((By.ID, locator_value)))
        element.click()
        element.send_keys(input_value)
```

Code explanation:

- We create a **Super Class** *BasePage*.

- The **function** *set_element_id* has two parameters: *locator_value* and *input_value.*

    The *locator_value* will take the web element's **ID** as argument and *input_value* will take any string input value as argument.

    set_element_id **function** waits (*please refer to section 3.4.2 for Explicit Wait*) and locates the web element whose **ID** is *locator_value*. After the element is found by its **ID**, the element is clicked using **click( )** method and a value *input_value* is send into it using **send_keys( )** method.

3.5.2: Locators

Locators contain list of IDs, class name, xpaths, link text, partial link text, css selectors of the entire web application.

- Open **Notepad++** -> create a new **python** file and name is *locators.py.*

(For demonstration purpose, I will be adding only few locators of our Tasty Food Delivery Service project.)

```
from selenium.webdriver.common.by import By
from selenium import webdriver
class CreatePageLocators:
    id_first_name = "id_firstName"
    into_para_class_name = "text"

class HomePageLocators:
    link_text_1 = "Create New Profile"
    heading_xpath = "//h1"
```

103

Code explanation:

locators.py file contains two classes, **Class** *CreatePageLocators* and *HomePageLocator.*

Class *CreatePageLocators* and *HomePageLocator* contain the list of web element's ID, class name, xpath, link text of *Create New Profile page* and *Home page* respectively.

.

3.5.3: Pages

Pages will contain list of methods or functions dealing with each element of the web page.

> **Please note:** Each page of the web application should have its own separate **Class** and this **Class** should contain the list of methods or functions which will hold the information about each individual components of the web page.

Now let's create separate **class** file for *Create New Profile* page (Link: http://sbasu.pythonanywhere.com/tastyFoodApp/create).

- Open **Notepad++** -> create a new **python** file and name it *createNewProfile.py*. This file will contain all the information of *Create New Profile* web page.

```python
from selenium import webdriver
from locators import CreatePageLocators
from element import BasePage
class CreateNewProfile(BasePage):
    def __init__(self,driver):
        BasePage.__init__(self,driver)
        self.driver = driver

    def get_title(self):
        title = self.driver.title
        return title

    def get_intro_text(self):
        intro_text = self.driver.find_element_by_class_name(CreatePageLocators.into_para_class_name).text
        return intro_text

    def firstName(self,val):
        e = BasePage(self.driver)
        e.set_element_id(CreatePageLocators.id_first_name,val)
```

Code explanation:

- Import **Parent Class *BasePage*** from ***elements.py*** file and the **Class *CreatePageLocators*** from ***locators.py*** file.

```
from selenium import webdriver
from locators import CreatePageLocators
from element import BasePage
```

Class ***CreateNewProfile*** is the **Child Class** of ***BasePage***
(To understand Python Inheritance , please refer to chapter 2, section 2.9)

- Function *get_title* gets the **title** of the web page and returns it.

- Function *get_intro_text* gets the introductory paragraph text from the *Create New Profile* page and returns it.

  > **Please note:** Instead of hardcoding the web element's **class name** into **find_element_by_class_name( )** method, we called the **class name** from *locators.py* file -> **Class** *CreatePageLocators -> intro_para_class_name.*

- Function *firstName* with parameter *val*, simply calls the *set_element_id ( )* function from its **super class** *BasePage* and pass *val* into it.

  > **Please note:** *set_element_id( )* receives the web element's **ID** from *locators.py* file -> **Class** *CreatePageLocators -> id_first_name*

  (*set_element_id( )* function code is present in section 3.5.1)

Now let's create a separate **class** file for *Home Page* (Link: http://sbasu.pythonanywhere.com/tastyFoodApp/)

- Open **Notepad++** -> create a new **python** file and name it *homePage.py*

```python
from selenium import webdriver
from locators import HomePageLocators

class HomePage():
    def __init__(self,driver):
        self.driver = driver

    def test_title(self):
        get_title = self.driver.title
        return get_title

    def test_heading(self):
        get_heading = self.driver.find_element_by_xpath(HomePageLocators.heading_xpath)
        return get_heading.text

    def test_link(self):
        get_link = self.driver.find_element_by_link_text(HomePageLocators.link_text_1)
        return get_link
```

Code explanation:

- **Class *HomePage*** will not be inheriting any property from **Super Class *BasePage***, so no inheritance is performed.

- **Function *test_title*** locates the **title** of the *Home page* and returns it.

- **Function *test_heading***, locates the **heading** of the web page and returns it.

> **Please note:** The web element's **xpath** is received from *locators.py file -> Class HomePageLocators -> heading_xpath.* (*code present in section 3.5.2*)

- **Funtion** *test_link* locates the **link** and returns it.

> **Please note:** The web element's **link text** is received from *locators.py file -> Class HomePageLocators -> link_text_1* (*code present in section 3.5.2*)

3.5.4: Test

In **Test**, we perform the actual test of the web page by accessing the methods or functions from **Pages**.

For example: The *Home page* of our *Tasty Food Delivery Service* project has its own *homePage.py file* (*created in section 3.5.3*). In order to test this page, it will have its own *test_homePage.py* file.

Before we create **Tests** for each web page of our project, let's first understand the basic structure of a **Test Case Class** depicted by the screen shot below:

```
import unittest
from selenium import webdriver

Class Test_Page1 (unittest.TestCase) :

    def setUp( ):
        # entry point


    def test_Page1( ):
        # test the page


    def tearDown)( ):
        # exit point


if __name__ == '__main__' :
    unittest.main( )
```

Important points to note are:

- We must import the **unittest module** and from this module include the **TestCase class**.

- The **setUp( )** method or function contains the lines of code which must execute **BEFORE** running the **test function**.

    This method contains tasks like: load the driver, open specific URL, implicit wait time etc.

- All **test** functions **MUST** start with prefix **test**.

- **tearDown( )** method or function will run at the **END**. This method is basically used to end the execution and exit out.

What does the below two lines of code means

if __name == '__main__':

      unittest.main()

I would like to explain this with a simple example.

Let's create a **python** file *test_CreateNewProfile.py* which will test the *Create New Profile* page.

test_CreateNewProfile.py file will contain the standard **setUp** method, **test** method and **tearDown** method and it will also contain the above two lines of code at the end. These two lines simply mean that if *test_CreateNewProfile.py* is running directly as the **main python** file and not imported from any other module then set the value of **python special variable __name__** equal to **__main__** .

Now **if __name__ == "__main__"** , then call the **main( )** function from **unittest** module.

What are unittest assert methods ?

Selenium Assert methods are used to perform certain checks and they should only be used within the Test Class.

Few most important and commonly used assert methods are:

110

1. assertEqual (*first, second, msg=error_message*)

This method checks whether the value of *first* matches with *second* or not. If it does not matches, then display the error message and fail the test.

2. assertNotEqual (first, second, msg= error_message)

This method checks whether the value of *first* matches with *second* or not. If it does matches, then display the error message and fail the test.

3. assertTrue(expr, msg = error_message)

This method checks whether the given expression *expr* returns boolean value true or false. If true PASS, if false return the error message and fail the test.

4. assertFalse(expr, msg = error_message)

This method checks whether the given expression *expr* returns boolean value true or false. If false PASS, if true return the error message and fail the test.

The screen shot below shows the **test case class** of *Create New Profile* page.

test_CreateNewProfile.py

```python
import unittest
from selenium import webdriver
import createNewProfile
class Testing(unittest.TestCase):
    def setUp(self):
        self.driver = webdriver.Chrome()
        self.driver.maximize_window()
        self.driver.get("http://sbasu.pythonanywhere.com/tastyFoodApp/create")
    def test_CreatePage(self):
        driver = self.driver
        home = createNewProfile.CreateNewProfile(driver)
        title = home.get_title()
        self.assertEqual("Create New Profile - Tasty Home Food Delivery Service",title,'
        intro = home.get_intro_text()
        self.assertEqual("Greetings, Please fill the form below to get enrolled into the
        home.firstName("kia456")
    def tearDown(self):
        self.driver.quit()
if __name__ == '__main__':
    unittest.main()
```

Code explanation:

- To test the *Create New Profile* page, we need to import the *CreateNewProfile* class from *createNewProfile.py* file created in section 3.5.3.

- **Function setUp( )** loads the driver, maximizes the window and opens the *Create New Profile* page.

- **Function test_CreatePage( )** performs the test.

```
driver = self.driver
```

*......Created **object** home **of class** CreateNewProfile*
```
home = createNewProfile.CreateNewProfile(driver)
```

*access the get_title( ) **method** from CreateNewProfile **class** and pass it into a variable title*
```
title = home.get_title()
```

check the value of title matches with the expected value or not
```
self.assertEqual("Create New Profile - Tasty Home Food
```

*access the get_intro_text( ) **method** from CreateNewProfile **class** and pass it into a variable intro*
```
intro = home.get_intro_text()
```

checking the value of intro matches with the expected value or not
```
self.assertEqual("Greetings, Please fill the form below
```

*accessing the firstName **method** and passing an argument "kia456"*
```
home.firstName("kia456")
```

- **Function tearDown( )** exits out from the test.

Now let's save everything and run the test file.

Open command prompt -> navigate to the *test_CreateNewProfile.py* file location and run the script using **python** command.

113

python *test_CreateNewProfile.py*.

```
 Getting Default Adapter failed.

----------------------------------
Ran 1 test in 8.838s

OK
```

The script ran successfully.

Now let's follow the steps above and create a Test Case **Class** for our *Home Page*.

test_homePage.py

```python
import unittest
from selenium import webdriver
import homePage
class Testing_HomePage(unittest.TestCase):
    def setUp(self):
        self.driver = webdriver.Chrome()
        self.driver.maximize_window()
        self.driver.get("http://sbasu.pythonanywhere.com/tastyFoodApp/")
    def test_HomePage(self):
        driver = self.driver
        home = homePage.HomePage(driver)
        title = home.test_title()
        self.assertEqual("Tasty Home Food Delivery Service",title,"title did not match")
        heading=home.test_heading()
        self.assertEqual("Tasty Home Food Delivery Service",heading,"Heading did not match")
        link_1 = home.test_link()
        self.assertTrue(link_1.is_enabled(), "Button is not enabled")
        link_1.click()
    def tearDown(self):
        self.driver.quit()
if __name__ == '__main__':
    unittest.main()
```

Code explanation:

- Import *HomePage* class from *homePage.py* file created in section 3.5.3

- **Function setUp( )** loads the driver, maximizes the window and opens the *Home* page.

- **Function test_HomePage( )** performs the test

```
def test_HomePage(self):
    driver = self.driver
    home = homePage.HomePage(driver)
```
*get the **title** using test_title( ) method and store it in variable title*
```
    title = home.test_title()
```
check the title matches with the expected title or not
```
    self.assertEqual("Tasty Home Food Delivery Service",title,
```
*get the heading using test_heading( ) **method** and check whether it matches with the expected heading or not*
```
    heading=home.test_heading()
    self.assertEqual("Tasty Home Food Delivery Service",headir
```
access the link using test_link( ) method
```
    link_1 = home.test_link()
```
check whether the link button is enabled or not using selenium is_enabled( ) method. It true PASS. if false, fail & throw error message
```
    self.assertTrue(link_1.is_enabled(), "Button is not enab
```
click on the link
```
    link_1.click()
```

- **Function tearDown( )** exits out from the test.

Now let's save everything and run our test script.

115

```
[1200:10624:1210/161741.6
d to read descriptor from
[1200:10624:1210/161742.1
73 Getting Default Adapter
.
----------------------------
Ran 1 test in 10.555s

OK
```

3.5.5: *Test Suite*

Test Suite is used to run all **Test Case Classes** together and by doing so the entire web application is tested end to end.

The basic structure of a Test Suite is:

import unittest module.......
import unittest

......import all the test classes...

import TestClassPage1
import TestClassPage2

.....get all the test methods from Test classes TestClassPage1 and TestClassPage2 using the following methods and store it in variable test_page1 & test_page2......

test_page1 = unittest.TestLoader( ).loadTestsFromTestCase (TestClassPage1)

test_page2 = unittest.TestLoader( ).loadTestsFromTestCase (TestClassPage2)

...create test suite by combining test_page1 & test_page2 and store it in variable test_suite using the following method............

test_suite = unittest.TestSuite ([test_page1,test_page2])

....run test suite using the following method

unittest.TextTestRunner( ). run (test_suite)

Important points to note are:

- **TestLoader( ) class** present in **unittest** module is used to load **test cases**.

- **loadTestsFromTestCase** loads all **test methods** from the **test class**.

- **run( )** method from **TextTestRunner runner class**, runs the test suite.

Now let's create a Test Suite for our project by following the above rules and structure.

- Open **Notepad++** -> create a new **python** file and name it *testSuite.py*

testSuite.py

```
import unittest
from test_HomePage import Testing_HomePage
from test_CreatePage import Testing

test_HomePage = unittest.TestLoader().loadTestsFromTestCase(Testing_HomePage)
test_CreatePage = unittest.TestLoader().loadTestsFromTestCase(Testing)

test_suite = unittest.TestSuite([test_HomePage,test_CreatePage])

unittest.TextTestRunner().run(test_suite)
```

Now let's run our code.

```
DevTools listening on ws:/
DevTools listening on ws:/
-----------------------
Ran 2 tests in 25.578s

OK
```

The test suite ran successfully.

3.5.6: How to generate a HTML report or a log file after running a Test Case Class

To generate a HTML report, we need to install **HTMLTestRunner**.

Open command prompt -> navigate to the **python** file location (*installed in Chapter 2 section 2.1*) -> **Scripts** -> then type the following command

pip install html-testRunner

```
C:\Python\Scripts>pip install html-testRunner
Collecting html-testRunner
  Downloading html_testRunner-1.2.1-py2.py3-none-any.whl (11 kB)
Collecting Jinja2>=2.10.1
  Downloading Jinja2-2.11.2-py2.py3-none-any.whl (125 kB)
     |████████████████████████████████| 125 kB 1.7 MB/s
Collecting MarkupSafe>=0.23
  Downloading MarkupSafe-1.1.1.tar.gz (19 kB)
Using legacy 'setup.py install' for MarkupSafe, since package 'wheel
Installing collected packages: MarkupSafe, Jinja2, html-testRunner
    Running setup.py install for MarkupSafe ... done
Successfully installed Jinja2-2.11.2 MarkupSafe-1.1.1 html-testRunne
WARNING: You are using pip version 20.2.3; however, version 20.3.1 
You should consider upgrading via the 'c:\python\python.exe -m pip 
```

The unittest testRunner is installed successfully.

Now let's look into a basic structure of a **Test Case Class** which uses **HtmlTestRunner** to generate a HTML report.

```
import HtmlTestRunner
import unittest

class Testing_HomePage(unittest.TestCase):

    def setUp( ):
        ..............

    def test( ):
        ..............

    def tearDown():
        ................

if __name__ =='__main__':
    unittest.main ( testRunner = HtmlTestRunner . HTMLTestRunner
( output = 'output_report_location_in_forward_slash' ) )
```

By following the syntax above, let's add the highlighted lines of code into *test_homePage.py* file created in section 3.5.4.

119

```
        link_1 = home.test_link()
        self.assertTrue(link_1.is_enabled(), "Button is not enabled")
        link_1.click()
    def tearDown(self):
        self.driver.quit()
if __name__ == '__main__':
    unittest.main(testRunner=HtmlTestRunner.HTMLTestRunner(output='C:/U..../selenium/selenium_project'))
```

Save everything and run *test_homePage.py* file

Unittest Results

Start Time: 2020-12-11 00:49:40
Duration: 9.07 s
Summary: Total: 1, Pass: 1

__main__.Testing_HomePage	Status
test_HomePage	Pass

Total: 1, Pass: 1 -- Duration: 9.07 s

The HTML report generated successfully.

Wish you all the best and thank you very much for buying this book.

Always remember, the most important learning is Self-Learning..

Printed in Great Britain
by Amazon